Faint Praise

Faint Praise

The Plight of
Book Reviewing in America

Gail Pool

University of Missouri Press
Columbia and London

Copyright © 2007 by
The Curators of the University of Missouri
University of Missouri Press, Columbia, Missouri 65201
Printed and bound in the United States of America
5 4 3 2 1   11 10 09 08 07

Library of Congress Cataloging-in-Publication Data

Pool, Gail, 1946–
    Faint praise : the plight of book reviewing in America /
Gail Pool.
        p. cm.
    Summary: "Pool's behind-the-scenes look at the institution
of book reviewing analyzes how it works and why it often fails,
describes how editors choose books for review and assign them
to reviewers, examines the additional roles played by publishers,
authors, and readers and contrasts traditional reviewing with
newer, alternative book coverage"—Provided by publisher.
    Includes bibliographical references and index.
    ISBN 978-0-8262-1727-1 (hard cover : alk. paper)
    ISBN 978-0-8262-1728-8 (pbk. : alk. paper)
    1. Book reviewing—United States.   I. Title.
    PN98.B7P66 2007
    808′.066—dc22

                                    2007014101

♾™ This paper meets the requirements of the American
National Standard for Permanence of Paper for Printed
Library Materials, Z39.48, 1984.

Designer: FoleyDesign
Typesetter: The Composing Room of Michigan, Inc.
Printer and binder: The Maple-Vail Book Manufacturing Group
Typefaces: Barbedor and ITC Minion

For Jeremy

Contents

Faint Praise

Introduction

The Reviewer's Lament

How many competent critics have we in America? Not many. The critical judgment furnishes the most notable jargon of the literary world. There is not a work of art worth noticing at all that does not use up, in its critical characterization, all the adjectives of praise and dispraise. . . . It is probable that incompetence, flippancy, arrogance, partisanship, ill-nature, and the pertinacious desire to attract attention, will go on with their indecent work until criticism, which has now sunk to public contempt, will fall to dirtier depths beneath it.

—*Scribner's Monthly,* March 1875

In America, now . . . a genius may indeed go to his grave unread, but he will hardly have gone to it unpraised. Sweet, bland commendations fall everywhere upon the scene; a universal, if somewhat lobotomized, accommodation reigns. A book is born into a puddle of treacle; the brine of hostile criticism is only a memory. Everyone is found to have "filled a need," and is to be "thanked" for something and to be excused for "minor faults in an otherwise excellent work." "A thoroughly mature artist" appears many times a week and often daily; many are the bringers of those "messages the Free World will ignore at its peril."

—Elizabeth Hardwick, "The Decline of Book Reviewing," *Harper's,* October 1959

*B*ook reviews first appeared in America at the end of the eighteenth century. They have been frustrating people ever since. So many essays and articles have been written lamenting the sorry state of American reviewing that they constitute a minor genre. For two centuries reviews have been lambasted by critics, often reviewers themselves, who have complained that reviews are profligate in their praise, hostile in their criticism, cravenly noncommittal, biased, inaccurate, illiterate, or dull. Generally, the argument runs, American reviewing has never been worse. I remember coming across a *Publishers Weekly* article in 1993 called "The Decline of Book Reviewing,"[1] the precise title of Elizabeth Hardwick's famous *Harper's* article, published in 1959, which made me wonder whether the field was in decline yet again or whether this was merely the latest stage in one long decline.

If book reviewing in America has declined, it is hard to say from what glorious pinnacle it has descended. The high point was probably not in 1987, when Andrew Greeley called reviews "self-important, pompous and supercilious," or in 1963, when John Hollander suggested, "Whatever is wrong with reviewing in America has been growing steadily worse." Most likely it wasn't in 1942, when Max Gissen in *Antioch Review* labeled reviewers "part of the publishers' selling force," in 1934, when Helen E. Haines in *Library Journal* spoke of the field's "engulfing and meaningless amiability," or in 1926, when Edmund Wilson observed that "it is scarcely possible nowadays to tell the reviews from the advertising." Undoubtedly, it was not in 1897, when the *Bookman* declared that "in no country is the current comment on books more lacking in thought and workmanship." It couldn't have been in 1875, when *Scribner's Monthly* predicted that "criticism, which has now sunk to public contempt, will fall to dirtier depths beneath it." And it was probably not in 1865, when the *Nation* spoke of American criticism's "promiscuous and often silly admiration," or in 1833, when the *Mirror* called it "worse than worthless. Weak tea and bread and butter—milk and water—we cannot think of anything stale, diluted, insipid enough for a comparison. . . . Nothing but puff." It wasn't in 1817, when reviewers were compared to cannibals, or in 1805, when they were chastised for their "lavish encomiums," and it couldn't have been much earlier: we're back at the start.[2]

Viewed in juxtaposition, these complaints—this "jeremiad concerning American book reviewing,"[3] as one cultural historian has termed it—can seem faintly comical. The venom. The scorn. That asymptotic decline! The charges are so excessive, so extravagant, they rest so shakily on the myth of a Golden Age of reviewing that clearly never existed that it's tempting to dismiss them as typical publishing fare. As anyone in publishing knows, it is a self-critical, gloomy, hyperbolic field, in which something is always judged to be in decline or dying, whether it's the novel or books themselves. As any reviewer knows, whatever one critic says is likely to set another's teeth on edge, the war between writers and reviewers is never-ending, and critics are likely to be reviled for what they do, however well or badly they do it. And as everyone knows, it's always satisfying to bring down those who we think have set themselves—undeservedly—on high. As the magazine historian Frank Luther Mott observed, "We should recognize that nobody loves the critics, now or ever."[4]

As a longtime reviewer, review editor, and columnist, I'm as familiar with this climate of complaint as I am with the complaints themselves. I'm aware that much of the carping is exaggerated, self-serving, and biased; that many reviews are intelligent, perceptive, and well written; and that it's easier to rail against "decline" than to grapple with the inherent problems in the field—the intrinsic difficulties of reviewing and the lack of cultural and economic support—that make certain shortcomings inevitable. All the same, I find myself joining the venerable tradition and sharing the critics-of-the-critics' sense of outrage.

Although it may seem old-fashioned to say it, and though I'm hardly a disinterested observer, I believe that book reviews matter. They matter not only to authors, publishers, and critics, those of us in the field whose livelihood and egos are involved; they matter not only to the readers who are trying to use them to guide their reading; they also matter to readers who don't read reviews. They influence reading. Even today, when reviews have been diminishing in number and alternative kinds of book coverage have emerged, hundreds of reviews appear weekly in newspapers, in magazines, and on the Web; our most prestigious publications continue to set our literary agenda. In certain areas, such as literary fiction and serious non-fiction, the books that receive attention tend to be the books that most people read—as individuals, in book groups, in schools. Reviewers' assessments indirectly help determine which books will win awards and which authors will be well published. Their commentary influences not only literary standards but also cultural attitudes, helping to shape what we think about many issues and whether we think about certain issues at all.

Yet we have only to look at our book pages to see that reviewing, in playing this role, fails in ways that can't be dismissed as trivial or excused as inevitable, that unacceptable practices—widely accepted in the field—routinely undermine the very reasons we read reviews.

Most of us—even reviewers—turn to reviews both to help us decide what to read and to find out what is out there to be read: we read reviews in our areas of interest, looking for recommendations, and we read reviews of books we have no intention of reading, whether to arm ourselves for the cocktail party circuit or because we truly want to be informed. We may also of course read reviews because we take pleasure in the play of ideas, or in reading about reading, or in the well-written review as a literary form. But essentially we want consumer advice and cultural guidance.

Yet how can we use reviews to make intelligent choices unless they describe books intelligently, placing them in some meaningful context and providing an accurate account of what they're about?

Reading nonfiction reviews, I want to know what the author said, how he arranged his material and laid out his arguments, how he arrived at his conclusions and what those conclusions were. Of what use are those many reviews that fail to describe the book at all, focusing instead on what I take to be its subject—though whether it really is its subject or simply what the reviewer wanted to talk about is something I can't assess, knowing so little about a book they haven't bothered to describe. How can I know what the book says when reviewers don't bother to attribute the information they're relating, omitting the simple, "In this book" or "As Joe Author says," and leaving me to wonder whether the reviewers independently know the often obscure—yet unsourced—things they're reporting, or whether they're merely appropriating them from the book at hand? And how am I to trust the accuracy of reviews when, if I should happen to read several reviews of a book, I find they disagree in their basic descriptions of the book's central message (Reviewer X: According to this book, "a mother's work is to stay home and raise her children"; Reviewer Y: The author "by no means urges that all moms stay home with their kids all day,"), suggesting that many reviewers practice the Rorschach method of criticism, and find what they're looking for.[5]

Reading fiction reviews, I want a description that reveals the bones of the story and suggests why the book is significant. How am I to use those many fiction reviews that consist almost entirely of plot summary, which don't tell me what a book is about, only—at length—what's in it, and which manage at once to bore me and to give away so much of the story they ruin my reading pleasure in advance? How does it help me grasp the novel at hand when reviewers, instead of providing some useful context, offer outlandish authorial comparisons: Can Ms. Author really be like Zola, Balzac, and Cheever?[6] Who would have dreamed that so many women writers were "like Jane Austen," so many short story writers "like Chekhov"!

Beyond description, if I'm to decide whether to read a book, I need an assessment—and one that seems clear, fair, and supported by the critique itself. Of what use is a review that offers no evaluation? Or provides one so qualified, so hedging, so apologetic for even mentioning the "minor flaws" (which don't sound minor at all) that I can't discern what the reviewer is really saying? Or delivers an opinion that sounds dismissively— and dismissably—hostile ("The man's books smell worse than newspaper wrapped around old fish."[7])?

And how can I believe the praise when there's so much of it and so much of it is over the top? On a single Sunday book page, *Boston Globe* reviewers declare that Michael Ondaatje, in *Anil's Ghost,* has created "a novel of exquisite refractions and angles: gorgeous but circumspect," that Rupert Thomson's *The Book of Revelation* has "that rightness that makes a work of art," that Leonard Michaels's *A Girl with a Monkey* is "uncompromising fiction. . . . They hardly make it like that anymore," and that Zadie Smith, with *White Teeth,* has "changed literature's future." The *Washington Post Book World,* reviewing Rick Moody's memoir, says that its "timeless exploration of issues that are essential to what it means to be an American makes it likely that *The Black Veil* will take its place among classic American memoirs"; *Boston Book Review* proclaims that Peter Carey's *True History of the Kelly Gang,* has "permanently extended the range of the English language"; and the online magazine *Salon,* reviewing Zadie Smith's *The Autograph Man,* says that a new book from this author "feels like an occasion to open up another chamber in your heart and another lobe in your brain to take it all in . . ." and that to pick up this book, "is to follow Dorothy as she steps out of her marooned, black-and-white Kansas farmhouse into the Technicolor splendor of Oz."[8]

The splendor of Oz? New chambers and lobes? How can I trust such assessments to guide my reading when most books, I find, are at best pretty good, and when I know how few books in a century change literature let alone the English language?

How am I to trust reviews at all when, in search of the reasoned commentary of the expert reader, the articulate coherence of the professional writer, the sophisticated insight of the professional critic, I find myself in a curious zone where the normal rules of language and logic don't seem to apply, a realm in which syntax, grammar, even meaning have strangely decomposed, and critical standards dissolved? A zone in which a *New York Times* reviewer, having just decisively panned Joyce Carol Oates's novel *Middle Age,* can somehow conclude: "Still, naked of a compelling plot, in a strange sense Oates's remarkable ability is clearer than ever. . . . Never mind that it's not much fun to read; you could still use *Middle Age* as a primer on how to write fiction."[9] A zone in which a *Boston Globe* reviewer can, incredibly, describe "credible complexity in a character" as being achieved in "at least two ways: Either distinctiveness is a matter of the sometimes gaudy and eye-catching methods of personality—stark red hair, deep sag to the breast, the tortured lisp of the poorly born—or it can be a presentation of the sometimes invisible but momentously significant suasions that inhabit us all—the 'not-thought' in thought, the unseen in the visible, the places into which the imagination must reach."[10] A zone in which a *Times* reviewer, discussing Jonathan Franzen's novel *The Corrections,* can remark, "Sure, I guess it's a no-no to put stuff in your book that doesn't pay off, but I can't scrape together much outrage when I'm basically having a good time," and further observe, "If you don't end up liking each one of Franzen's people, you probably just don't like people"[11]— leaving me to wonder whether I can really be reading a major review in our leading newspaper or perhaps a freshman theme.

Finally, and perhaps above all, how can I use reviews as a cultural guide unless they do let me know what is "out there" and assure me that the books they've chosen to discuss are the most worthy of discussion? What do I do when, turning to our larger newspapers, especially the largest, the *New York Times Book Review*—the only general-interest publications with review sections sufficiently sizable to reflect what's being published—I find that the selection of books is extremely limited: that most of the titles are published by a small number of large commercial publishers, with only a handful of university and small press books reviewed in briefs, tucked away in the back, in corners, or in roundups; and that while certain kinds of book are heavily represented and some authors reviewed everywhere, whole categories of books tend to get short shrift—books on the arts, foreign literature, serious cultural criticism, even travel, entire genres are meagerly represented, while innovative fiction and poetry are largely ignored. Is it plausible that so few books from small and university presses are as significant as those from larger commercial houses, or that books on so many topics just don't happen to be worth a review?

Do I go searching elsewhere for reviews of university or small press titles—in the *New York Review of Books,* for example, or *American Book Review*—when I can't imagine why I would have an interest in such books in particular or how such books form an intellectual category? (Don't university and small presses publish all kinds of books?) Do I go searching for specialized reviews, of art books or poetry, in print or on the Web, though I haven't really all that much interest in those subjects and only want to know which books in all subjects, including those two, are worth my attention? Or do I just stay with the mainstream reviews, aware that they aren't supplying cultural breadth, that they aren't identifying the books that are best or matter most, that often they're reviewing books that, according to the reviewers, don't seem to matter at all, leading me to question why a book page has wasted a chunk of its limited space, as well as my time, and to brood on what books they—and I—have surely missed.

How can it happen that such a serious enterprise works so badly that it often fails to work at all?

Reviewing is a slippery subject. It's even a slippery word. The term *reviewing* refers at once to a literary field and a business, a system and an individual endeavor, a process and a multitude of very different products. Although we tend to talk about "reviewing" and "the reviews" as if everyone were on the same book page, I'm not sure that everyone is. Even limiting the discussion to reviews written for a general audience—ignoring specialized reviews for professional audiences, and television and radio reviews with oral traditions of their own—the field that remains is large and unwieldy in its diversity. There isn't even agreement on what constitutes a review.

Everyone, I'm sure, would call the critique on the book page of the Sunday newspaper a book review. But what about the reader commentary on a bookselling site such as Amazon? The book site itself calls these reviews.

And while "A great read!" as a total commentary wouldn't in anyone's estimation qualify as a review, some of the write-ups certainly read like the reviews that we find in our newspapers. Yet some people deny them the same status. Is the issue that they're written by "amateurs"? In fact, our newspapers have always been filled with reviews by amateurs, many of whom are unpaid, and no one has ever denied that what they've written are reviews.

And what about the long essay in the latest issue of *Lit'ry Quarterly* on the works of A. S. Byatt? Is this a review, or is it literary criticism, and how do these differ, if, in fact, they do? While some people reserve the term *literary criticism* for the academic world, many people use it more loosely to connote a higher quality of book commentary, a critique that has scope, depth, and complexity, that discusses a book within the context of a genre or the author's total oeuvre. When Martin Amis, in *The War against Cliché*, remarks that John Updike's reviewing is "high-powered enough to win the name of literary criticism," he seems to be suggesting that reviewing, if it is good enough—"high-powered" enough—can turn into literary criticism, which is different in quality but not in kind. But Victoria Glendinning in her essay "The Book Reviewer: The Last Amateur?" suggests that the two are different activities, that reviewers aren't *critics,* a term she reserves for academia, and really shouldn't be called critics, though she is comfortable with the term *literary journalist.* And Peter S. Prescott, the longtime book commentator for *Newsweek,* finds a place between the literary critic, at one end of the spectrum, and the book reviewer, at the other, for someone he calls the "book critic," who occupies the "middle ground."[12]

Some of these distinctions seem to me too vague to be useful: at what point does a review become good enough to be called literary criticism, where's the line, who decides, and what purpose does the distinction serve? Some appear to be class distinctions: as we would all rather be travelers than tourists, we would all rather be critics than reviewers, and "real" reviewers rather than mere readers having our say. None of this answers the question of whether in critiquing books for the Sunday paper, for the literary quarterly, or for Amazon, we're doing the same or different things, and which, if they're different, we should call "reviewing."

Part of the problem, as Joseph Epstein says in his essay "Reviewing and Being Reviewed," is that "it has never been quite clear what the purposes of a book review are. Should a review grade the author, passing out complaints and criticism along the way? Should it chiefly perform a service for readers, informing them whether the book under review is or is not a waste of their time? Or should it combine both tasks, an aid to both writers and readers?"[13] Some people argue that evaluation should be the primary aim of a review. But according to W. H. Auden, "The principal duty of a reviewer . . . is not judging or explaining, but describing. What he ought to say is, 'I have just read a book sent me by its publishers. Let me tell you the kind of book it is, so that you can decide if it sounds like the kind of book you would like to read.'"[14]

Clearly in a field that is short of definitions, I need some distinctions if I'm to talk about reviewing at all.

Historically, what has distinguished reviewing from other kinds of critical commentary is that it deals with new books. Reviewing only emerged in the eighteenth century as the number of published books increased, and the reading public grew. Although the word *review,* as a noun, appeared as early as 1649, according to the *Oxford English Dictionary,* the verb form, as I'm using it, first appeared in 1781—"I would never review the work of an anonymous authour," wrote Dr. Johnson to Mrs. Thrale—and in 1783, we find Cowper writing, "I am reviewed, and my book forwarded in its progress by a judicious recommendation." In her essay "Reviewing," Virginia Woolf suggests that toward the end of the eighteenth century, a split in the field of criticism occurred, resulting in two distinct lines with two distinct functions: "The critic," she writes, "dealt with the past and with principles; the reviewer took the measure of new books as they fell from the press."[15]

Most simply then, in talking about reviewing, I'm talking about one kind of criticism: the criticism of new books. We review a new book by A. S. Byatt, but we do not "review" a book by Jane Austen—the very sound of it is wrong. If the Byatt essay in *Lit'ry Quarterly* examines her new book against the backdrop of her earlier work, it is a review—or an essay review; but if it examines all her work when no new book has appeared, it is a kind of criticism but not a review.

Woolf's reference to "principles," as Glendinning suggests, points to yet another kind of criticism which is distinct from the reviewing for a general audience that I'm talking about (though, to confuse things, it may sometimes deal with new books, and it can be called reviewing): academic criticism. The difference isn't only that academic critics address a specialized audience and write in a jargon incomprehensible outside their field ("tropes," "semes"), while reviewers address a general audience and write in a jargon everyone understands ("compelling," "luminous"). More to the point, the academic critic examines books through the prism of theories, descendants of Woolf's "principles," while the reviewer, though not necessarily unprincipled—the charges against them notwithstanding—is like H. L. Mencken's empirical critic, conducting "his exploration with whatever means lie within the bounds of his personal limitation. He must produce his effects with whatever tools will work. If pills fail, he gets out his saw. If the saw won't cut, he seizes a club."[16]

Simple as they are, these two basic distinctions—new books and a lack of theory—determine the nature of reviewing, both its central tasks and its intrinsic problems. Because review editors are dealing with new books, for example, in deciding what to review, they're working not with a canon but with unknown quantities and need to find ways to discern which titles might have value. Because reviewers are dealing with new books, they're writing for an audience that hasn't yet read the books they're discussing, which is why not only an evaluation, but also an accurate description is such a necessary part of the review; without description, no assessment can make sense.

Because reviewers are dealing with new books, which they must do while the books are still new, they inevitably lack time for reflection. And they're grappling with books that have no history. Unlike the critic writing about James Joyce's *Ulysses,* who, whether he thinks it succeeds or fails as a work of art, already understands its impact, the reviewer working in the present has no such knowledge; he's trying to perceive not only what is good and what he likes, but also what will last and what will matter. While critics writing about the past are considering books that have been mulled over many times and can draw on a variety of ideas in arriving at their own, reviewers, writing about books that almost no one has read, lack the discussion, the argument that helps clarify opinion, and the validation that encourages confidence and even originality. As John Simon has observed, "Some of the best critical formulations have been made against previous ones, and, let's face it, you cannot play squash without a wall."[17]

And because reviewers, unlike academic critics, lack an acknowledged framework that they and readers share, their readers don't really know on what basis they're forming their judgments. This isn't to say that reviewers have no basis. The reviewer who says, "This novel fails to move me," or "This novel is dull because it has no strong story line," clearly believes that a novel, to be successful, should be moving or have a strong narrative. But unlike predetermined theories, these ideas about books vary from reviewer to reviewer, and they sometimes vary for the same reviewer from book to book. It becomes part of the reviewer's job—within what is usually very little space—to encapsulate an entire viewpoint not only on the book under review but on the subject, so readers can gauge where the reviewer is coming from and whether they're likely to agree with what he says or think him wrong.

How and how well editors and reviewers handle these intrinsic problems—how they choose books, how they treat them—comprise the basic issues I am interested in dealing with. Whether particular reviews are right or wrong in their judgments—an ever-popular topic—is not among them. As a basis for judging reviews, 'right' and 'wrong' is a tricky measure. Accuracy can be evaluated in terms of errors, fairness in terms of evident bias, coherence and style in terms of dangling thoughts and participles. But assessing critical judgments inevitably comes down to taste. And it would lead my discussion astray: the question of whether Ms. Reviewer is right or wrong to call Mr. Author's novel "good" would involve an extensive discussion of what I think a good novel should do. But my focus is on what I think a good review should do.

In any case, to judge reviews right or wrong seems to me reductive. Not only does it eliminate the variable of taste, it too often diminishes the review to a single dimension: the verdict. As readers we tend to be focused on the verdict. "Did he like it?" we want to know as we read the review. We jump to the last paragraph, which may determine whether we'll read the book and even whether we'll read the review.

But a good review is more than a verdict. It's an essay, however brief, an argument, bolstered by insights and observations. A review that proves over time to be "wrong" in its judgment may be valuable for those insights and observations, while a review which proves to be "right" in its verdict can be right for foolish reasons.

In his introduction to *Rotten Reviews,* for example, a compendium of critical comments from reviewers who got it "wrong"—having "unjustly trounced" books we now admire—Anthony Brandt asks: "Who would want to have called *Wuthering Heights,* not too long after it had appeared, 'a crude and morbid story'?"—as Henry James apparently did.[18] But it is Brandt here, not James, who seems to me to have got it wrong. As much as I happen to like *Wuthering Heights,* I would find it hard to deny that it is a crude and morbid story. That the novel has endured doesn't disprove that. It suggests that many people either like or at any rate don't mind the crudeness and morbidity or find that other aspects of the book more than compensate. But for some readers nothing can compensate for crudeness and morbidity, and for them *Wuthering Heights* could never be considered a good novel. A contemporary critic would have to address the novel's lasting power—as James did not—but by characterizing the book accurately, he did his job well (not surprisingly), both as a critic and as a reader's adviser, preparing his audience for the book they would find.

If *reviewing* is a slippery word, it becomes still more slippery when we consider that it refers not only to literary journalism but to journalistic criticism of every kind: art, popular music, classical music, movies, theater, dance, television—all are reviewed. And all share a world that has undergone changes in recent years, changes that have posed a challenge to traditional reviewing.

In 2004, "Reporting the Arts II," a study by Columbia University's National Arts Journalism Program, reported that between 1998 and 2003, the majority of newspapers reduced the number and size of their articles about arts and culture, and "with few exceptions, papers almost everywhere" were "devoting more of their arts space to listings." The survey also reported that newspapers were turning increasingly to freelancers, syndicators, and wire services for arts coverage.[19] During these years, not only newspapers, but also newsmagazines and even cultural magazines reduced their book review space as well. In the meantime, a great wave of critical opinion on everything from the newest Bach CD to the latest Tom Cruise movie has emerged on the Web.

In their introduction to "Reporting the Arts II," the editors observe that newspapers, in covering the arts, have generally navigated "between two extremes." The traditional model, as they suggest, "emphasizes the paper's filtering role," promising readers: "Our experts will select the most noteworthy artistic productions and elucidate their importance, meanings, strengths and weaknesses for you."[20] In recent years, newspapers have been tending toward the other extreme, offering listings and basic "capsule information" and letting readers decide for themselves. Many editors, they suggest, are "pushing for a third kind of arts journalism," consisting of "arts news reporting, as distinct from criticism."[21]

The immediate impact of these trends has already generated concern among journalistic critics. They have seen the loss of staff positions and writing opportunities and have expressed dismay at "coverage" replacing and sometimes commercializing criticism. Writing in the *Boston Globe*, arts critic Bill Marx took a stand against the intensified use in theater and movie reviewing of the "feature/review," a hybrid that he called an "insidious way of converging art and commerce, of transforming criticism into publicity." As space has shrunk, reviewers in all fields have lamented the diminution of their critical role. As John Simon, writing at the time about movies, said: "Reviewing has become largely simplistic consumer guidance, with the broader, more speculative view rarely in evidence and decreasingly in demand."[22] The many articles on the theme "everyone's a critic" chronicle the response to the Web's many self-appointed critics competing with traditional reviewers in an era when cultural authority has already been challenged.

How all of this will play out in the long run is not yet clear, and the impact is likely to differ for the various forms of journalistic criticism as these forms differ from one another. Book, art, popular music, classical music, movie, theater, dance, and television critics are writing for different audiences, they are often writing with different aims, they are working in fields with different economies, and they face different tasks. Unlike book reviewers, for example, movie and television critics are writing for a mass audience. Unlike book reviewers, who are dealing with relatively low-cost and—with some exceptions—low-profit items, movie and theater critics are dealing with productions that may be extremely profitable, extremely costly, or both. And unlike book reviewers, art, music, movie, and performing arts critics are consistently dealing with art, if not high art: most reviewers of nonfiction books, whether about government, medicine, or education, are not. Such factors influence everything from the level of advertising support a particular kind of criticism might earn, to its cultural impact and centrality, to the writing style a particular kind of critic might use.

For book reviewing, some form of traditional model, whether in print or online, seems to me crucial. For books, listings—even within a category or genre—are useless; we may as well read *Books-in-Print*. Capsule summaries are scarcely better: for either cultural or consumer advice, of what use is a brief abstract of a novel? And "news" is of limited value. Opinion is needed, and as the surge of opinions on the Web makes clear, it is very much in demand. Whatever the format and whatever the technology, we need book reviewing that plays "a filtering role"—and plays it well.

A question that hovers over my analysis—perhaps any analysis—of what is wrong with book reviewing is what can be done to improve it. Those complaints after all have been circulating for decades, and though the critics of reviewing at times forget to mention it, the inherent problems in the field are hard to resolve. What appear to be straightforward problems—overpraise, undernotice, bias—turn out to be complex. Reviewers have the byline, and they have generally taken much of the blame. But this is a large and disorderly field. Editors and publishers, authors and readers also play their roles. Literary traditions, cultural attitudes, the demands of both the marketplace and the genre play theirs. I would have to be naive or dishonest to claim I could put this house in order, that analysis and a few suggestions are enough. But I believe we can do better than we do. And the starting point is surely to understand why bad reviewing happens despite good intentions and how so many intelligent people who love books can say so many unintelligent things in their behalf.

Unnatural Selection

Of making many books there is no end.
—Ecclesiastes, 12.12

But the inventions of paper and the press have put an end to . . . restraints. They have made every one a writer, and enabled every mind to pour itself into print, and diffuse itself over the whole intellectual world. The consequences are alarming. The stream of literature has swollen into a torrent—augmented into a river—expanded into a sea . . . Unless some unforeseen mortality should break out among the progeny of the Muse, now that she has become so prolific, I tremble for posterity . . . Criticism may do much; it increases with the increase of literature, and resembles one of those salutary checks on population spoken of by economists. All possible encouragement, therefore, should be given to the growth of critics, good or bad. But I fear all will be in vain; let criticism do what it may, writers will write, printers will print, and the world will inevitably be overstocked with good books. It will soon be the employment of a lifetime merely to learn their names. Many a man of passable information at the present day reads scarcely anything but reviews, and before long a man of erudition will be little better than a mere walking catalogue.
—Washington Irving, "The Mutability of Literature." *The Sketch-Book,* 1819–1820.

At a National Writers Union conference many years ago, I served on a panel called "Becoming a Household Name: Book Publicity and Reviews." My role as the reviewing member of this panel, with its dual agenda of pragmatism and dreams, was to answer the question on the mind of every writer in the room: How do I get my book reviewed? The difficulty of my task was to be honest without being entirely depressing about the difficulty of theirs. Had I been frank, I would have suggested they think hard about a nom de plume, say Anne Tyler or Philip Roth.

More than 150,000 books are published in the United States each year. From this tidal wave of print, only a tiny fraction will be reviewed in the mainstream press, the review space authors most want. By recent estimates, the *New York Times Book Review* and the *Washington Post Book World* each review around 2,000 books a year, and the *Los Angeles Times Book Review* between 1,000 and 1,500—and these are the country's largest book sections. Most newspapers review far fewer titles, and the total has been dwindling as newspapers themselves have diminished in number. General-interest magazines, whether in print or online, don't begin to make up the deficit, reviewing, at most, a few hundred a year. And the percentage of books reviewed is smaller than these numbers would suggest, since there is considerable overlap among all book sections—mainstream, small press, Web—and a popular biography, a best-selling memoir, or anything by a well-known author like John Updike will receive multiple reviews.

It would be nice to think that the few titles chosen for these coveted spots are the worthiest. After all, to review insignificant or mediocre books while missing important or outstanding ones undermines good publishers, depresses good authors, demoralizes reviewers, and cheats readers. No aspect of reviewing matters more. Yet the editor who relies on the tools and traditions of the trade is bound to make poor choices, giving attention to undeserving books and overlooking better ones.

Any discussion of selection has to begin with those numbers: over 150,000 books and room for reviews of, say, 500. No other arts review editors deal with comparable figures. Film releases, for example, number only in the hundreds—according to the Motion Picture Association of America, 549 new films were released in 2005, up from 520 in 2004,—[1] and a restrictive form of distribution means that many films won't even play in particular locations across the country and thus aren't choices for review in publications serving those areas. By contrast, online bookselling has made an extraordinary percentage of books published—and even self-published—easily available for all. On what basis does the book review editor decide? Are certain subjects more important than others? Is fiction more worthy of notice than nonfiction? And is this to be decided by editorial fiat or by sales figures? Does he seek out the best books, the most important ones, the most influential? The study of madrigals that is well researched, exquisitely written, beautifully produced; the scholarly history of cartography that may make a difference in understanding how people have seen the world; or the clumsily written but provocative book on presidential politics that may affect polls? Does he choose the excellent novel that may sell 3,000 copies or the poorly written thriller that will sell 1,000,000? Should the book page educate taste or cater to it?

In making these decisions, no editor is working from a blank slate. If the book page is part of a larger publication, as most are, the books reviewed will usually reflect the aims of its parent, with whom it shares an audience. Newspapers cater to a broad, disparate, mass audience defined by locality, and traditionally they have been the primary source of reviews for most readers. Their book page editors are under pressure to make their selection varied, accessible, and politically evenhanded, and not to miss the "important" books. They're expected to take an interest in local authors and issues: The *Washington Post Book World* pays more attention than most papers to political books; the *Boston Globe,* as the largest paper in New England, keeps its eye on the region; at the *Cleveland Plain Dealer,* as a columnist, I was asked to choose Ohio writers' books for review and to give some preference to Midwest authors in general.

Magazines, by contrast, cater to a discrete group of subscribers defined by interest, education, and income, and their literary editors will look for books suited to their particular audience. Review editors of publications that have a political or cultural agenda will choose books that fit within it. Independent review publications can follow their independent aims, but their subscribers will expect to find what they paid for and what they've found before. Thus the *New Republic*'s literary editor will look for culturally and politically sophisticated books; the *Nation*'s literary editor may seek out books of interest to its left-wing readers; the *New Criterion* will choose titles of interest to cultural conservatives, even liberal books its readers will especially loathe (and will count on seeing panned). Online, *themysteryreader.com* will review crime fiction, while *Bookreporter.com* will look for "great reads."

As they whittle and cull to arrive at their allowable quota, editors are also guided by broader traditions in the field. Print reviewing has a long-standing commitment to quality—no "Account of Books that are Trifling,"[2] as *The History of the Works of the Learned,* founded in 1699, declared of its criticism—and newspapers and magazines have tended to avoid mass-market fare. Popular categories they do review, such as mysteries, are generally relegated to roundups of short reviews. That this tradition is still at work seems evident in publications' policies about the kinds of books they automatically won't review, not simply because the subject matter doesn't fit with the publications' editorial aims, but because editors believe these books aren't likely to meet their editorial standards or fit the higher-quality image they wish to project. In a recent National Book Critics Circle survey, the kinds of books editors frequently identified as out-of-bounds included self-help, New Age, romance—all categories that are considered intellectually and literarily lower class—and, pretty much across the board, self-published titles, a group that is burgeoning and changing these days but that still carries the stigma and the problems of the vanity press, whose books no one but the authors need approve. Editors know that any automatic exclusions will inevitably eliminate worthy books. But they calculate that these categories contain such a high proportion of unsuitable choices the losses will be small relative to the time gained to focus on more likely candidates. And in view of the numbers, any automatic decisions are bound to be a relief.

Refining these general aims and policies, which aren't carved in stone—which aren't usually even written on paper—are the interests, biases, and taste of a publication's review editor, who decides not only which books will be reviewed but also the kind of space and position they'll receive: which books will get a lead review, a long review or a short one, which will be assigned to a roundup. Editors are likely to have their own visions of what an ideal book section should be. They'll certainly have their own opinions on books and current publishing—none of us would be in this field if we didn't—and will want to put their individual stamps on book pages by giving more space to authors, subjects, or kinds of books that they think matter and less to those they think have been overplayed.

But whatever their aims and ideals, editors will face an obvious dilemma in trying to achieve them. The only way to select what they themselves think are the best or most important books, the noteworthy novels or biographies or travel books, is to read them. And this, of course, they can't do. Most editors are working alone. While a very few review editors—at the *New York Times Book Review,* for example—have staff to help choose titles, others have no one even to help do battle with the book mailers, which arrive in exhausting numbers. And who can read 150,000 books? Admittedly, the actual starting number is smaller. Many of the books published are textbooks or specialized titles that a general book page wouldn't review. And since, by convention, publishers bring out their books mainly throughout two big seasons, fall and spring, and book pages, by convention, review books only within their publication season—indeed, as close to the publication date as possible—review editors are only looking at a portion of the total production at any one time. No matter. The figure could be 30,000. It could be 15,000. It's still an unreadable number of books.

Moreover, while this time frame suits publishers, who are eager to drum up some fanfare for their newest entries, and periodical publishers, who are eager to give a newsy air of currency to their book pages, and authors, who are excited about their latest efforts, and booksellers, who are eager to return low-selling titles as soon as possible, it's a schedule that puts enormous pressure on editors. Allowing time to receive books, assign reviews, get reviewers' copy and edit it, they need to make their first-cut decisions so far in advance that they're dealing with books they not only haven't read but haven't even seen. Editors are forced to rely upon secondhand information, much of it insufficient, biased, or inappropriate, about the nature and quality of the books they're selecting or rejecting for review.

For review editors, the primary source of early information—for some books their only source—is the publisher, who sends out a variety of materials, which may include catalogs, press releases, press kits, personal letters, advance reading copies or galleys (i.e., early uncorrected proofs of the work) and finally the book itself. Needless to say, none of this material is disinterested. Publishers are as aware as review editors of the number of books published and the intense competition for review space; part of their job is to win that competition. They need to make their books stand out. Everything they send is promotional, even the book, which carries blurbs or endorsements from the most impressive names the publisher can attract. Contrary to what some people think, these blurbs aren't paid for, and unlike certain notorious movie blurbs, they aren't invented, but they are carefully solicited from an author's supporters—colleagues, former teachers, friends—and even the most honorable will not present a hard-edged assessment of the book.

Publishers' catalogs, even before they're opened, have conveyed a crucial piece of information: the name of the publishing house. Readers don't generally pay much attention to the name of a publisher. I doubt most readers, if you asked them, could identify the publishers of the books they're currently reading, though nearly every book would carry the company's name and colophon—or logo—on both the spine and the title page. Those colophons are quite distinctive: Knopf's Borzoi is probably the best known. But readers, understandably, identify books by title and author; no one says, "I'm reading a new novel from Knopf," nor do they ask at a bookstore for the latest biography from Random House. Only a few publishers, such as Penguin, in its time, or, in a quite different vein, Harlequin, have so identified themselves with a particular kind of book and physical design that readers have known and bought their books by the publisher.

Review editors, however, are very much aware of publishing houses. They do speak of a new novel from Knopf, or a new biography from Random, or "interesting new work" from Counterpoint. Review editors identify publishers by category: large trade house, small press, university press; they identify them by the kinds of book they tend to publish: serious fiction or nonfiction, popular fiction or nonfiction, genre; and they identify them by the quality of their lists, quality both of content and of production. These identities change over time, and many of the long-established publishing houses have lost their familiar personalities as they've merged into conglomerates and attempted to diversify their lists. But even within the conglomerates, individual imprints and editors can sustain an identity, as do smaller publishing houses, where editorial and fiscal decisions may be made by one or two people.

The degree to which the identity of a publisher influences selection will vary from editor to editor, publisher to publisher, and book to book. Like so much in this field, that influence is impossible to measure. It may be that Knopf gets as many reviews as it does because it has so many good books. But there's no question that editors will open a catalog from a respected publisher like Knopf expecting to review books from its list, willing to trust the quality of its books and to schedule them before they've even seen them, whereas they'll approach a catalog from a less respected or well-known publisher without such an expectation and far less willing to take a chance on their books. An unknown author's first novel from a small press may be superior to the one from Knopf, but unread, the two aren't equal. This inequality might be to some degree diluted if the editor could at least see early galleys of the small press book. But small presses are sometimes unsophisticated about the need to send galleys or can't afford to send galleys that aren't requested—or even to print up galleys at all—and by the time they send a finished book, the review space may already have been assigned to the book from Knopf.

The catalogs themselves, which are sales, marketing, and promotional tools all in one, are designed not only to inform editors about books, but also to position the books culturally and commercially. At the most basic level, they announce when books will appear; describe them (generally in glowing terms); place them in a ready-made category (biography, fiction, politics, etc.); provide a brief bio of the author, including birthplace, residence, prizes won; and include endorsements. For editors, who are scanning the catalog mainly for subjects and authors, all of this is necessary information, the basis on which they can decide whether they have any interest in or obligation toward a book at all.

But beyond this, the catalog also informs editors which books have most importance in the publisher's list. Just as there are lead reviews on a book page, there are lead books in a catalog, which are placed up front, which may have longer write-ups, glitzier graphics, and more publishing details—the size of the print run, the extent of the advertising budget, the scope of the publicity, the schedule of the book tours—that indicate the degree to which the publisher will be pushing these titles. The promotional material sent out for specific books, often accompanying the galleys, reinforces the hierarchical information in the catalog. All books receive a press release, but books the publisher is promoting more strongly may also get a glossy media kit, with photos, author interviews, early reviews, and so forth, encased in a shiny folder, or an assortment of paraphernalia (an "evidence kit" for a mystery, for example, or buttons), some of it inventive, some of it fatuous. Unlike the catalogs, which are used by editors, this material will be passed along to the reviewer and includes author information the publisher hopes will be helpfully favorable in framing a review. Editors aren't fools, and they are unlikely to be swayed in making choices or forming opinions by the content of such material. But neither are publicists fools: they know that editors won't miss the message they're sending about which books will be most heavily promoted.

In deciding whether or not to pay special attention to lead books and others that will be highly publicized, review editors are aware that these aren't necessarily the best books. Publishers may consider a particular book they're pushing excellent, or they may be hoping to earn back its large advance, offered on the basis of a proposal or an author's reputation long before the book was written. What earns a book its high budget is more likely to be sales potential than editorial excellence. But sales potential matters for the review media as well. Editors will have to question whether they want to ignore books that will be advertised widely, displayed boldly in bookstores, promoted in interviews or television book clubs, celebrated in book features, and probably reviewed in other publications, whose editors will be pondering the same question. The decision to review these "bigger" books might be more than just jumping on a bandwagon; I've worked with editors who felt an obligation to inform their readers about the quality of books they would be aware of and were likely to be curious about, and who hoped to present an honest critical viewpoint on those books. In any case, if editors choose them, they're selecting books that may not be worthy of attention, limiting the space for books that might be more deserving, and letting publishers make the real decision about which books get reviewed.

Some of the information from publishers is not only promotional but personal as well. Recommendations for specific titles may arrive in the form of notes or calls from publishers, editors, or publicity directors, or perhaps visits from publishers' sales representatives, who woo review editors at publications with larger or more desirable book sections. If the advocates are people whose taste the editor respects, their recommendations may be welcome; they have actually read the books and, if they're biased, they should have no reason to be more biased toward one of their books than the rest other than an actual preference. Review editors know which book editors or publicists they can rely upon for good advice. In her online newsletter, "Holt Uncensored," Pat Holt, former book review editor at the *San Francisco Chronicle,* writing on the death of one of the Norton sales reps she came to know, spoke highly of sales reps in general, a group who, "with their irreverent humor and easy pragmatism, their love of books and their ferocious respect for booksellers," could help ensure that the book page editor didn't miss "a local author or a literary gem or even an obvious heavyweight coming up for publication."[3]

But however endearing or respected, none of these people can be impartial; they're selling books. And even when the recommendation comes from someone whose taste the review editor doesn't particularly respect, she's still under some pressure to heed it. If publishers want reviews, review editors depend upon publishers to send information early and to send the books themselves and to send them on time. This is a field where relationships matter.

In the play for media space, where all communication is in some sense promotional as well as informational, the large commercial houses outplay small and university presses by communicating more. By sending more galleys and books, by providing more catalogs, press releases, and press kits, by developing and using a larger publicity staff, they create a strong presence which is hard for review editors to ignore—and which most editors don't ignore enough. Advertising has often been credited with winning more review space in the mainstream press for the large trade houses, and it's true that these houses are more likely to advertise and that historically their books have benefited. The links are self-evident. But this other, equally commercial, promotional presence has always been strong and helps explain why even today, when most book pages are bereft of advertising, books from the large houses are more often chosen for review.

If publishers are the primary source of early information about books, review editors can also turn to a secondary source, one with its own virtues and risks: the trade press. Such publications as *Publishers Weekly, Kirkus Reviews, Booklist, Library Journal,* and *ForeWord* offer prepublication reviews that briefly describe and evaluate thousands of books, often indicating titles they consider of special interest or value by means of starred or boxed reviews. Trade reviews aren't intended for the general reading public, and most readers probably aren't familiar with them. But they're crucial to a book's success. They're published for booksellers and librarians, who rely on them to decide what books to order and in what quantities they'll be needed. Unless a book is reviewed in the trade magazines, it will have a hard time finding its way into libraries, bookstores, or—since review editors use them as well—the book pages of the general press.

From the review editor's perspective, these reviews are extremely useful in whittling down the number of books to be considered. Editors can trust that in the culling most of the truly unreviewable books have been omitted, and that in the large remaining number—*Kirkus* reviews some 5,000 titles a year, *Publishers Weekly,* around 7,500—it is unlikely that a masterpiece has been missed. And the information they provide is more disinterested than the information provided by publishers.

But these magazines are published for a different audience, and in using them to make their own decisions, review editors are using tools designed for a different purpose. Library publications are edited for librarians, whose selection decisions take in a range of factors of little relevance to review editors in the general press, such as the way that people use libraries and the kind of books patrons expect to find. Bookselling publications are edited for bookstores, whose selection decisions depend largely on sales. *Publishers Weekly* is the trade journal of the publishing industry and is edited to serve not only booksellers but publishers. If all review editors are dependent upon publishers for information, books, and ads, *Publishers Weekly* is dependent on the field for its very identity; it has a commercial investment in the well-being of the field, which depends upon selling books, that renders its role as impartial critic dubious.

Trade magazines, in addressing booksellers and librarians, are designed to help audiences that have to stock even mediocre and bad books because their patrons want them. A bookseller who decides not to carry John Grisham's best-selling legal thrillers because she thinks he has a tin ear isn't doing her business a service; a librarian who decides not to carry Danielle Steel's extraordinarily popular romances because she thinks Steel writes execrable prose isn't doing her taxpaying patrons a service. And a trade magazine that doesn't review these books isn't doing its audience a service. All need to let their readers know the books are available and provide them with a description that they can use, in turn, to describe the books to their patrons.

That trade magazines have an obligation to review these books doesn't mean they have to praise them, and often they don't. *Kirkus* in particular has a long-standing reputation for scathing critiques. Even *Booklist,* which only reviews books it recommends, will indicate that certain titles are recommended with qualifications and should be purchased by libraries only as demand requires. But in view of these publications' aims, too much praise is inevitable. The majority of books are mediocre, but it won't help librarians and booksellers for trade reviewers to say that, since many of these books ought to be in libraries and bookstores anyhow—if they purchased only masterpieces, their shelves would be empty; and once a reviewer is recommending a book for purchase, it would be foolish—and sound foolish—to use his three hundred words telling readers why the book isn't any good.

Review editors aren't under the same obligation to devote their far-more-limited space to books they consider bad or poorly written solely because they're likely to sell well. They can do this, of course, but they have other options. They can look for books that are exceptionally good as well as likely to be popular, books that are exceptionally good but not likely to be popular, or books that may be bad but matter. But identifying these amid the thousands that receive general praise in the trade magazines isn't easy. What stands out are the reviews that are boxed or starred. But for review editors to simply make these their own top choices as well is to let their selection be determined by other editors and reviewers about whom they know little (in fact, reviewers in some of the trade publications are anonymous) and who are approaching books from a different perspective.

The conflicts for review editors are clearest in *Publishers Weekly*, which is the trade publication they are most likely to be reading since it offers not only weekly reviews, but also spring and fall forecast issues, publishing news, articles on current trends that are filled with statistics, and the latest gossip and book buzz, all of which help keep review editors abreast of what's happening in the field. In September 2000, *Publishers Weekly*'s editor-in-chief, Nora Rawlinson, announced that the reviews would be adding a new "Forecast" paragraph to "discuss the commercial potential of a book, beyond the quality of the content itself." In addition, she said, the reviews themselves would pay more attention to market potential. "Forecasts" would address such points as "likely audiences for the book," "the market health of the book's subject or genre," "the author's track record," "pricing, when it may affect a customer's purchase decision positively or negatively," "cover appeal," and "events that may bring attention to the book, including movies."[4] This market-conscious approach to books is quite pertinent to what *Publishers Weekly* should be doing, but it veers sharply away from the criticism that is wanted on a general-interest book page. Review editors who rely too heavily on the news and reviews in *Publishers Weekly*—and in my experience, it's hard to escape the magazine's influence—may find themselves devoting more space to well-positioned books than to well-written ones and covering literary events more than literature.

Whether they're using material from publishers, the trade forecasts, or gossip and news, review editors in the early stages of selection will inevitably be dealing with information that has been shaped by other people's needs. The quality of their book pages depends on how they use the information to suit their own needs. What are their aims? What are they looking for? Unless their premises are sound, even reading the books won't lead to a first-rate set of choices. The *New York Times Book Review* has editors who help screen books, and yet its selection has for many years now been disappointingly limited.

As editors sift through titles, sorting them into the definite reviews, the definite discards, and the possibilities, they're likely to be considering not only their publications' editorial aims, their personal interests, and each book's quality (to the degree that they can discern it), but also its popular appeal. Although one editor I worked with viewed Herodotus as beach reading, most editors take a somewhat less literary view. They may want worthwhile books, but they want books that will draw readers as well. Unlike trade publications, which, however much they may compete with one another, together have a captive audience of book buyers, the book page in the general press does not. The review editor, addressing an American audience that buys few books and will read about them only if its interest is aroused, is under pressure to find titles with a subject, or an author, or some literary or extraliterary buzz that will arouse it.

Among the definite discards are those mass-market books they reject as a matter of policy, which may have appeal—they're certainly what many people are reading—but which are prejudged to be inappropriate. At the other extreme, American media are wary of anything that sounds too intellectual, or, in the arts, difficult. In his essay "The Film Critic of Tomorrow, Today," J. Hoberman says of movies, "In no medium is the stigma of the 'difficult'—which ranges from the absence of stars to the presence of subtitles—more damning."[5] Yet the stigma seems to pertain to books as well. Review sections in newspapers, in general-interest magazines edited for mass audiences, and even in more select magazines such as the *New Yorker* share this wariness. They leave nonfiction titles that sound too intellectual to a few magazines, such as the *New York Review of Books* or the *New Republic*, or the academic quarterlies, and fiction that might be difficult—i.e., innovative—to literary and arts reviews. There are exceptions, of course, individual review editors and columnists who make an effort to deal with more challenging books. But overall there is a quest for the middle ground that leads mainstream editors, once again, to rely upon the large commercial houses that are aiming to attract the same broad audience they themselves are seeking and to avoid the risk of university presses whose general-interest books might not be sufficiently general or the small presses whose literature might be too literary.

From the first—from the earliest glimpse of the catalogs—there are some titles that, good or bad, will by tradition be reviewed. Books by major and leading authors—Philip Roth or Margaret Atwood—will not only be automatically selected, they will, if they're substantial, almost certainly be assigned a prominent position, generally the lead. Since these decisions are made without regard to quality, they're obviously based on other assumptions: that books by major authors are in themselves so noteworthy that they warrant full discussion, that the book page serves as a literary record and should cover such authors, that readers are sufficiently interested in these authors to want to read in-depth about each of their efforts, that such books have value even if they aren't especially good—and of course they may be good, review editors hope they have a better chance than most books of being good. And at least, as the editors face a vast array of unknowns, they know something about these books. At a practical level, editors know that names draw readers, and names can be used to attract other celebrated names to review them, thereby enhancing these choices with double recognition and appeal.

Relatively few books, though, are automatically in or out. Most fall within the great mass in the middle, for which decisions need to be made. For these, editors will read between the lines and peer behind the words of every catalog, press release, and prepublication review, speculating on how a book will measure up to its description and to what they're looking for. As editors scan for possibilities, for books that they will send for, they're likely to seek out choices they think will minimize their risk. The author of several well-received books (or even one), the author who has won an award, the author whose work editors themselves have previously enjoyed is a known quantity and has an edge over the newcomer, who is a shot in the dark. The newcomer who has a classy publisher, personal recommendations, a prize, or impressive endorsements—especially from people who seldom give endorsements—has an edge over the newcomer who has only a book. Editors look for subjects that are perennial draws— the Civil War, historical biographies. They look for subjects that sound interesting—because they're topical (presidential politics in an election year) or entertainingly quirky (a book on the color *mauve*) or the focus of a dozen new books and apparently "hot" (a cluster of books on the television series "The Sopranos"). They watch out for what other book pages are doing, especially the *New York Times Book Review,* and if a book they rejected receives a rave elsewhere, they may assign it.

But these methods of minimizing risk are of dubious value. The author of two previous novels may be a known quantity, but her new book isn't, and it may be mediocre. Awards are unreliable. Endorsements are often biased, self-serving, or dishonest. Books that sound interesting may not be interesting at all. The book the *Times* reviewer said she loved can turn out to be a dud.

And the best of plans can go awry. A book the editor sent for really does appear to be excellent but languishes for want of the right reviewer; not all publications have the reviewer expertise available to the largest publications, and the editor who immediately needs someone knowledgeable about Woodrow Wilson or clinical depression may be out of luck. A book the editor sent for, which he expected to be excellent, turns out, upon arrival, to be awful; the publisher's catalog neglected to mention the author's unreadable prose. Or perhaps a book the editor sent for doesn't arrive at all.

The failure of publishers to send the requested books is a long-standing mystery in reviewing. Editors, after they peruse the catalogs, request the books they definitely plan to review, the automatic choices, and also the possibilities they're seriously considering. For these possibilities, final decisions will often be made only with book in hand, when editors have a chance to assess if not read it. This perusal will be only moderately helpful with fiction, where even preliminary assessment takes time, and quick judgments can easily be wrong, but an experienced editor can quickly size up at least the basic quality of nonfiction. Editors follow standard procedures for requesting books, generally sending in the checklists that accompany many catalogs or making individual requests. And books come, masses of them, but not necessarily the ones they sent for. While some editors are wooed by publishers, others are ignored.

Surveying review editors in 1984, Robert Wyatt, the book editor of the *Nashville Tennessean,* observed in a *Publishers Weekly* article called "Book Page Editor Blues" that editors located outside New York complained that publishers made it difficult to obtain review copies or failed to send them on time, while some editors at small-circulation papers said publishers failed to send them at all. Wyatt's own complaints echoed those of a previous book editor of the *Tennessean,* Donald Davidson, who wrote, in an article called "Criticism outside New York," more than fifty years earlier:

> The literary editor's task is not lightened at all by the system, or rather the lack of system, which a great many publishers use in sending out review copies. . . . Some of the publishers—especially the older, more conservative houses—studied rather carefully the peculiarities of the local page; but these were few enough. We always had a plethora of books that were not worth reviewing or that we were not interested in reviewing—a book of Yiddish hymnology, or a history of Gloucester, Massachusetts, or the speech defects of schoolchildren in a Brooklyn high school, or German diction in singing. And we were always missing important books, frequently books of local interest, for no intelligible cause, and being greeted, upon complaint, with a formula—"Our supply of review copies is exhausted," or a quarrelsome "Our records show that this book was sent you . . ."[6]

Davidson describes receiving Polish and Scandinavian novels from a publisher who didn't send a novel by a writer from Tennessee and being "refused a review copy of the diary of President Polk," whose tomb was located a few steps outside his office.

These complaints are borne out by my own experience in the eighties and nineties. Sending for books for a small but venerable library publication, I encountered a mix of disarray and belligerence, from the publicist who claimed a book I'd requested wasn't her publisher's (until I questioned why, then, the title was listed in their catalog) to those who treated me as if I might be planning something underhanded, perhaps selling their books to the well-known review-copy table at the Strand Book Store. When, as a reviewer, I suggested a title to the *Boston Globe,* the editor agreed, provided I could get hold of the book myself, a nonstandard practice in a field that, for ethical reasons, tries to keep reviewers and publishers apart, but a last resort for the editor who'd had such trouble with that particular publisher (Morrow, as it happens) that he simply wasn't willing to engage in the struggle.

Disorganization may account for the book that arrives, after three requests, in triplicate, too late to be reviewed. Carelessness may account for the publicist's ignorance of her own list. The lowly position of the publicity person who sends out books may account for the fact that by the time the book is ready to be sent, that person has often moved on—up, we may hope—to another position, leaving the request unfulfilled. But the hostility with which publishers sometimes meet editors' entreaties and their failure to address the problem make it clear that there is also disregard for publications that are small or "out of town" in a New York–centered field. Whatever the reasons for publishers' unresponsiveness, the very purpose of the book page is undermined if editors, in the absence of the books they've chosen, are forced to review the books they just happen to have.

As a guide, as cultural commentary, even as journalism, the book page takes its caliber from the caliber of the books it reviews. Too often the discussion of selection seems focused on whether mainstream publications should be reviewing more serious titles or more popular ones. But the more essential question is whether the titles being reviewed are worthwhile books, which can be found in any category. The challenge is to identify them. There is no way I would minimize what the review editor is up against in managing this. But neither would I minimize the inadequacy of our methods and the traditions the field seems to cling to no matter how often they fail.

By choosing books without regard to quality, review editors will inevitably find that they have often given their most prominent space to mediocre books. And since, as any reviewer can testify, it's difficult to write a worthwhile review of a book that isn't particularly worthwhile, editors will find a large portion of their book page is mediocre as well. By automatically giving long reviews to books by leading authors, whether or not the books are worth it, editors with little space will often find they have almost none left for works that may be far better.

By defining "mainstream" as narrowly as our general press clearly does, review editors almost guarantee the kind of dullness that prevails on so many book pages. Having rejected many of the books that, good or bad, have substance and are interesting to talk about because they seem "heavyweight" or too literary, the review editors choose the same kinds of books from the same presses, whose editors are publishing books characteristic of those houses, which is to say much the same as those they published before. Although, with the number and extraordinary range of our publications, every book page could be different from every other book page every week of the year, readers learn about yet another dysfunctional-family memoir, yet another "poignant" coming-of-age story, yet another book by an author we've previously read about and didn't think so highly of before. Readers may well feel as though they've already read these reviews. They may feel they've already read these books.

By defining "mainstream" commercially—by press—review editors sustain artificial cultural divisions and relegate certain publishers and authors to literary ghettoes. Newspaper readers don't learn about their books at all. By ignoring so many kinds of books, they encourage mainstream publishers to ignore them as well, to play it safe and publish what will be reviewed. By focusing so largely on the big houses, the leading books, the familiar, editors forfeit their chance to discover the new, to expand not only readers' awareness but the cultural mainstream itself.

Disturbingly, the level of overlap in our mainstream reviews, the tight focus on a relatively few books and few kinds of books, seems to confirm that editors are making the best choices, that there is general agreement on what the most significant books are, that these books are rising because of their own virtues. Some books do deserve the attention they get. But since editors are relying on the same sources of information, since they're working under the same commercial, cultural, and practical pressures, and, most important, since they're adhering to the same reviewing traditions, it's not surprising that they arrive at many of the same choices; it would be surprising if they didn't. What is confirmed is not the value of

the books but the consistency of the system and the discouraging confor-
mity of the trade. I know that people in the field claim that if a book is
outstanding, it will be reviewed. But I find it hard to see how anyone can
say this with confidence when most books published in America disappear almost unnoticed, and we have no way of knowing what we've
missed.

Vermin, Dogs, and Woodpeckers

"Reviewing" work is too badly paid for any reasonable being to think of making it either an art or a business.

—*Idler*, 1894

. . . The prolonged, indiscriminate reviewing of books is a quite exceptionally thankless, irritating and exhausting job. . . . The reviewer . . . is pouring his immortal spirit down the drain, half a pint at a time.

—George Orwell, "Confessions of a Book Reviewer"

The reviewing of novels is the white man's grave of journalism; it corresponds, in letters, to building bridges in some impossible tropical climate. The work is grueling, unhealthy, and ill-paid, and for each scant clearing made wearily among the springing vegetation the jungle overnight encroaches twice as far.

—Cyril Connolly, "Ninety Years of Novel Reviewing"

. . . And the absolute dregs . . . write for the Books Pages. Why? Because it's the lowest form of journalism there is. And the lowest form of that is reviewing fiction. You don't have to go out and discover things for yourself. You don't have to sit at the end of a telephone line. You don't even have to know anything about the subject. All you have to do is read a couple of hundred pages of someone wanking their imagination, and write five hundred moderately clever words about it.

—Amanda Craig, *A Vicious Circle*

Critics are like horse-flies which hinder the horses in their ploughing of the soil.

—Chekhov, as reported by Gorky, in *On Literature*

A critic is someone who enters the battlefield after the war is over and shoots the wounded.

—Murray Kempton

*B*ook reviewing in America is a hybrid occupation. Part trade and part profession, part art and part craft, part literature and part journalism, it lies somewhere between the outskirts of the work world and the fringes of the world of letters.

As a job, it has little to recommend it. The work is hard, the position insecure. As a "freelancer," I felt anything but free. I was always hustling, waiting for editors to call, taking on books I had little interest in reading because I needed the work, and the reviewer who declines too often may not be asked again. Whatever I wrote had to please the review editor, and the review editor's editor as well, an obscure figure whom in most cases I'd never spoken to and couldn't even have named. Most writing in America pays badly, but reviewing has a scale of its own, with fees far lower than people outside the field would believe. As a columnist, I might well put forty hours into scanning twenty books and reading four or five for a one thousand-word critique of three for $250 (reprint fees included). If this is near the minimum wage, it is somewhat higher than the going rate for reviewing. A recent National Book Critics Circle Survey showed that newspapers standardly pay from $100 to $400 for a review. And while the glossy magazines may pay considerably more, some publications pay even less, and some pay nothing at all, though they do promise a copy of the book (and often renege on that promise, leaving the reviewer with only a flimsy set of galleys). Of course, it could be worse: had the IRS carried out its onetime threat to tax that barely resalable book at full value, some reviewers would actually have paid to do their job.

Yet the job has its advantages. As a reviewer I can work at home, in the comfort of my study: I can avoid the commute, the noisy office, the moods and interruptions of colleagues. I can dress as I please. Books are delivered to my door, and I can send out my work easily these days, by e-mail: I needn't even face the weather. I can set my own hours, work early, late, or through the night, in long stretches or brief snatches, on weekends. And as work, reviewing can be extremely satisfying. To analyze how a book elicits its response is intellectually demanding and rewarding. To write so concisely that a few well-chosen words become an essay is an aesthetic triumph. To help others understand the nature and value of a particular book feels useful; and the commentary itself seems important, a contribution to thought and taste.

In terms of status, though, the reviewer's position is ambiguous. Like all published writing in America, reviews enjoy prestige, and reviewers, especially if they write for well-known publications, are widely regarded as wielding power.

But the prestige is limited. "Book reviewing," said the writer Guy Davenport, "is the slum of American letters"[1]—hardly a tony address. Reviewers have been compared to vermin, dogs, woodpeckers ("who, instead of enjoying the fruit and shadow of a tree, hop incessantly around the trunk, pecking holes in the bark to discover some little worm or other"[2]), and most often—and perhaps worst of all—failed writers. Who are the reviewers, according to Coleridge? They "are usually people who would have been poets, historians, biographers, etc., if they could: they have tried their talents at one or at the other, and have failed."[3] "Who is the book reviewer?" asked the mystery writer Andrew Greeley. The reviewer's credentials, he says, "often seem to be that he is a copy editor for the paper, or a reporter or a 'freelance journalist' or a 'novelist' (of whose books you've never heard)."[4]

As for power, it's the publication that has the power, the publication, if it is read, that sells books, the publication that will most often be cited in those blurbs that appear on book jackets and in advertisements which quote the review but so often fail to identify the reviewer: it isn't my name but that of the *New York Times* or the *Plain Dealer* that matters. My own power often seems confined mainly to elating or depressing an author and is even then begrudged as unearned, undeserved, and abused. An old literary cartoon depicts the epitome of this abuse: In the first of five frames, we see a man—middle-aged, balding, portly, glasses on nose, pipe in hand—reading in his armchair. In succeeding frames, he is absorbed in the book, he finishes it, he gazes out at us, clearly moved; a tear runs down his cheek. Turning to his desk, his expression now stern, he tosses aside his pipe, and leans into his typewriter: "The latest work in James McMurphy's oeuvre," he writes, the reviewer suddenly revealed, "is a pretentious and ill-conceived exercise in maudlin sentimentality burdened by a turgid and plodding prose style, a forgettably pedestrian plot, and feeble-minded attempts at wit."[5]

Dishonesty, meanness, failure—these are images that I as a reviewer have to bear. But in exchange, I obtain what the thousands of reader comments on our bookselling sites—and in the margins of uncountable library books—suggest every reader truly wants: a public forum for my opinions about books.

It isn't surprising, in view of its rewards that, despite its drawbacks, reviewing is a popular field: editors don't lack for reviewers. In response to another National Book Critics Circle survey several years back, the book editor of the *Atlanta Journal-Constitution* said she had "so many good freelancers already on board, someone has to really knock my socks off to get my attention"; the book review editor of the *Raleigh News and Observer,* though "keen on finding new talented contributors," observed that "like most editors, I have far more reviewers than space to print their work"; and the deputy editor of the *New York Times Book Review* noted that "interested freelancers" should be aware that the *Times* has a list of "hundreds of potential reviewers, many with published books to their credit, awaiting a first assignment."[6]

But neither is it surprising, in view of the drawbacks of the field, that despite this abundance of reviewers, there is a shortage of good reviews.

Who are our reviewers? The question, peculiar to reviewing, would make no sense in other fields: our doctors are our doctors, our teachers our teachers, our lawyers our lawyers. But reviewing pays so little, most reviewers are forced to earn their living in other ways. As befits an anomalous field, the workforce itself is anomalous.

Traditionally, reviewers have been characterized as falling into two groups: professionals and amateurs. The professionals are those who do make a living in the field—a few hardy freelancers, but mainly those who are affiliated with a single publication and are salaried: the chief critics, the columnists, the review editors, who, in addition to being editors, review. This has been a diminishing group in recent decades. The amateurs, reviewers who earn their keep in other ways, include the experts solicited for their expertise, the occasional reviewers who review because they enjoy it, the vast number of individuals who have maintained our local book pages for years and, as one editor observed, have included "college presidents, editors, lawyers, judges, insurance and bond salesmen, authors, clubwomen, housewives, clergymen, gentlemen farmers, army officers, teachers, politicians, and of course college professors."[7]

But this division, like most such divisions, doesn't quite cover the ground. Falling somewhere between the two groups are the reviewers who, though they may earn most of their living elsewhere—mainly as instructors or professors—review so frequently that it seems to me they have to be considered in some sense professionals. Falling outside both groups, nowadays, are the reader-reviewers who contribute to our bookselling Web sites—most notably Amazon—or who set up reviewing Web sites of their own. Most of these reader-reviewers comment, or review, only occasionally, for a book they particularly want to talk about, or as a favor for a relative or friend, or perhaps to satisfy a grudge against a rival or hated former teacher. But some review in such quantity, producing hundreds—even thousands—of reviews that publishers have begun to send them galleys, soliciting their opinions. These online reader-reviewers have been heralded as "amateurs." But what distinguishes them is not that they're amateur—they may well be professional reviewers in their other lives. Unlike our traditional amateurs, however, they're self-published: no editor has asked them to review, screened them for qualifications or biases, edited or approved their work.

These reader-reviewers who declare themselves qualified and hold forth raise the question of what gets anyone hired to review and—a separate question—what makes anyone qualified. Reviewing after all is not a credentialed field: no degree or special training is required. No schools that I know of award certificates or diplomas for reviewing. And while it's true that nowadays some writing and media programs offer courses in reviewing, this is a recent development and doesn't seem as yet to have had an impact on the field. Editors responding to the National Book Critics Circle survey, when asked what they looked for in reviewers, didn't mention giving preference to reviewers who had taken such courses, nor have I ever seen a contributor's note that said, "Joe Reviewer took Reviewing 101 in the Writing Program at X.U." Specialized schooling has yet to become a requirement or even a practical benefit in the field.

In fact, reviewing is an easy field to enter. It's true that most editors hire reviewers on the basis of their previously published reviews, and newcomers will somehow have to publish a few reviews so they will have samples, or "clips," to send to an editor if they want an assignment. But acquiring clips isn't terribly hard to do. The publication in which reviewers first appear doesn't have to be prestigious: they can review for their alumni/ae magazine, which is likely to welcome their work. More typically, they can review for local publications, perhaps a small literary magazine (my own port of entry many years ago), or newspapers, which, as they favor the books of local authors, often favor the work of local reviewers as well. If the potential reviewer is shrewd, and aware that he needs to work in advance, he will seek out forthcoming titles in such trade magazines as *Publishers Weekly* or *Booklist* (which are available behind the desk of any library), identify a title which is a likely candidate to get assigned in his local paper (perhaps because it has a local connection) and unlikely to have already been assigned (perhaps because it hasn't a famous author), and persuade the book editor to assign it to him.

The assignment, if he gets it, will almost certainly be "on spec," that is, offered on speculation with no guarantee that the review will be published or that he will receive compensatory payment—a "kill fee"—if it isn't. But once assigned, the review, if it turns out to be decently written, is likely to run. Book editors respect their assignments; and if the editor has planned for it, its absence will leave a gap in his book page. And if the review turns out to be better than decently written, the writer might well be offered another assignment. He will soon have several clips to send to other book editors as well, who, if he is persistent, will eventually respond. He has now become a reviewer.

In this process, as with self-published reviewers online, it is generally the reviewer who initially decides that he is qualified to critique books. Unless he has some particular area of expertise, he will presumably have decided this because he considers himself an astute reader, feels that he has something to say, and believes that he can write. Most of us believe these things. He will be aware from reading the brief bios that accompany reviews that other reviewers do not for the most part have more specific qualifications than he has. Along with the rest of the world, he may feel that they make a hash of it and that he can do it better.

It is one of the curious aspects of this field that though people deplore the poor quality of reviewing, no one seems to conclude that so many reviews are bad because reviewing is hard to do well. On the contrary, the faults are ascribed to the individual reviewers, and the attitude prevails at all levels of the literary world that reviewing is easy, something anyone can do. "Have you ever thought it would be fun to get paid for reading the latest books, and then for saying what you think of them? Then maybe you should think about reviewing books,"[8] suggests an article in *Writer Magazine,* sounding faintly like the offers on matchbook covers. In ambitious literary circles reviewing is viewed as an entry-level position, as Norman Podhoretz has observed, "a job for young men on the make: you serve an apprenticeship as a reviewer and then you move on to bigger and more ambitious things."[9]

Editors, for their part, are open to new reviewers, out of need, generosity, or the optimism required for the job: though well aware that not everyone can review, they know that just as any book in a stack of brand-new books might be terrific, anyone in the reviewing queue just might turn out to be an excellent reviewer, and that there's no knowing beforehand who will excel. There is no guarantee that the novelist will be better than the college president or the professor better than the housewife. Editors are willing to give writers a chance that might pay off for the book page as well. What they mainly look for in considering new reviewers or a particular review is good writing, which is often all they have to judge by (they can't assess the evaluation of a book unless they've read it), which can, in fact, be a valid indicator of good reading, and which is, in itself, a central concern: editors want their book pages read, and bad writing isn't much of a draw.

Indeed, editors put such emphasis on writing that another route to becoming a reviewer, besides writing reviews, is to publish something else. The author of a book who applies to review has a good chance of getting an assignment, and he may not even need to apply: editors often solicit reviews from authors, especially if they're celebrated writers whose names might bring status and readers to the book page, or, in newspapers, if they're local writers, particularly if their books have done well.

What is evident about this process is that qualification plays an uncertain role in hiring: the reviewers who are published may be qualified to critically assess books and explain their assessments, or they may not. Ideally, reviewers should be well educated, widely read, culturally aware, endowed with good memory and, needless to say, good taste. They must be able to read critically, think lucidly, and argue logically. They must write clearly enough to be accessible, sharply enough to be entertaining, and tightly enough to turn seven hundred words into an article. They need sufficient independence of mind to form their own opinions, sufficient confidence to stand by them, and sufficient courage to see them in print.

Ideally then—and such a description is very ideal—this is what the editor should be looking for. Some of these qualities obviously can't be checked for beforehand, though their presence or absence will be borne out over time. But review editors know far less about the people they hire than they might and certainly less than other employers know.

Although a 2006 National Book Critics Circle survey indicated that some review editors ask potential reviewers for a resume, many do not. As a reviewer, I was never asked to submit a resume. I wasn't asked about my educational background, not even where I went to school or what I had majored in. I wasn't asked for an overview of what I had read or my opinions about it. I wasn't asked for references, and only once, at the *Christian Science Monitor,* did a book page editor interview me—and that was for a column on magazines. As an editor myself, I followed this pattern of no-inquiry; to have demanded such information would have seemed inappropriate, a bit rude, in a field that didn't require it. Like most editors, I asked for clips.

If editors in this traditional hiring process can have little idea how well potential reviewers meet the ideal, the enterprise itself doesn't necessarily favor reviewers who do. It favors writers with an entrepreneurial bent, though this has nothing to do with critical or writing ability: not only must freelancers market themselves for their first assignments, they must continue to do so to broaden their contacts, to get new and better assignments, to move on as editors, publishers, and book pages change. It favors writers with a journalistic temperament that enables them not only to work quickly to meet deadlines, but also to tolerate the editorial standards of newspapers, where prose is likely to be sloppily copyedited, afflicted with typos, and variously chopped and mangled as "space" requires, though this may eliminate some writers too concerned about careful writing.

And because the process emphasizes writing as if it were a monolithic skill, editors often end up with reviewers who write well but may not be good critics, and authors whose skills may be entirely inappropriate. There is no reason to expect that the qualities necessary for good reviewing will be found in writers whose work doesn't call for them. This is especially evident in the many weak reviews by fiction writers that fill our book pages. Fiction writing requires very different skills from critical writing, and while a writer might have both, as did V. S. Pritchett, it's more likely that, as Edmund Wilson observed, the novelist, "though gifted and expert in his own field, may have no aptitude for or practice in reviewing."[10]

Fiction writers don't necessarily have a good analytical sense of why a piece of literature succeeds or fails, which is the most useful aspect of the review for the reader. Unless the reviewer can explain why a book works or doesn't, and unless his reasons are of value, his judgment has little meaning. The fiction writer is more likely to read, and to review, from the author's rather than the reader's perspective, focusing his attention on how the author solved certain writing problems; and there is always the risk that, in reading the book, he will be comparing those solutions to choices he himself would have made, which will color his judgment. While his own experience of being reviewed might bring a welcome compassion toward his fellow author, it can also soften his judgments, which may be further softened—indeed, rendered spineless—by the caution he feels as he looks forward, with trepidation, to seeing his own future books reviewed.

In hiring authors because they are authors, review editors are turning to writers whose main interest isn't likely to be reviewing: most fiction writers, poets, and biographers are primarily interested in writing fiction, poetry, and biography, not devoting the best of their energy and attention to criticism. Still worse, editors run the risk of hiring writers whose motive for reviewing is not to evaluate the books at hand but to promote their own names and their latest works, which are carefully mentioned in the contributors' notes. In a hilariously brazen scheme advanced online, a promotional guide suggested to authors that in order to promote their own books they should review books on Amazon: "The more frequently readers see your name, the more books you'll sell," the guide advised. "If you review a good number of popular novels by bestselling authors, your name and book title will be seen thousands of times."[11] The guide further recommended that the "overall tone" of these reviews should be positive and virtuously suggested that writers only review books they had actually read. Like so much of what we find online, this reflects openly, and rather shamelessly, a form of self-promotion that we have long had, somewhat better disguised, in print.

What we most need, both the reviewing community and readers, are critical writers who see reviewing as their work, who see themselves primarily as reviewers, a "professional literary class, distinct, on the one hand, from the journalist and popular novelist, and, on the other, from the damned professor,"[12] as Stuart P. Sherman, literary editor of the *New York Herald Tribune* more than fifty years ago, once suggested. But the question, said Sherman, was "how to develop and reward" such a class. This is a question we haven't answered today. Reviewing requires a combination of talents, skills, and knowledge—both broad and particular—that is hard to come by. Edmund Wilsons will always be rare. That the teachable qualities—critical reading and writing—are neither widely taught in our schools nor rewarded in our society, where the very word *talent* seems reserved for "creative" abilities, means that even the people who have the aptitude to acquire them very likely won't. And conditions in the field neither nurture nor encourage those who do. On the contrary, the situation is hardest on those with talent who want to apply it to reviewing, who want to take the work most seriously, who see reviewing as their vocation.

From a financial perspective, for example, fees may be equally low for all reviewers. But for the occasional reviewer or the amateur, who earns a living elsewhere, the reviewing fee comes as an addition to a paycheck, something small perhaps but extra. For most fiction writers and almost all poets, reviewing fees, even if they're only honorariums, will probably surpass the fees they receive for publishing their creative work in periodicals, which frequently pay their writers in contributor's copies of the publication.

But for anyone who wants primarily to be a reviewer, the fees are entirely impracticable. They force reviewers to take other jobs, diminishing the time they can put into the extensive reading they should be doing—either in general or as background for particular books—and into the careful thinking and incisive writing that reviews require but so often lack. If reviewers become book page editors in order to earn a salary but still remain in the field, they will find that the job entails demanding administrative and professional duties that are often only obliquely related to criticism. To begin with, they'll have to deal with their own editors and publishers, whose relationship to, and possibly whose view of, the book page will differ from their own, and who control the budget. They'll have to deal with publishers and publicists, cultivating good relationships while maintaining an ethical distance. They'll have to deal with the books, not only the time-consuming act of selecting those to be reviewed but the ordeal of getting them from publishers and the physically wearing task of grappling with the book mailers.

Most of all, they will have to deal with reviewers, who present an intricate set of relationships with needs and demands that can't be ignored: even reliable reviewers face personal crises that make them late; even good reviewers turn in lousy reviews; and even thoughtful reviewers often forget that they are among dozens with whom the editor has to be in touch. As an editor, I found that for many freelancers, I was their main contact with the literary world, the person who made them feel part of that world, and they expected me to fulfill the role by talking with them about books. From my perspective, such contact compensated them for the dismal pay, and in my experience editors who fail to engage with their reviewers seldom elicit their best work. But those who do will find, as I did, that their own time for reading and criticism is seriously curtailed.

While the occasional reviewer has the option of focusing on a single book, the economics of the field require that almost all professional reviewers will have to review too much. This can affect not only the way they write, setting them firmly on the road to hackdom, but the way they read. The goal becomes to read efficiently. For me, the best method of reviewing was always to read a book through once just to experience it as a reader, and then to read it again, taking notes, formulating my opinions. But by the time I had two columns, which entailed reviewing at least eight books a month, I felt under pressure to start the process from the moment I opened the book, immediately taking notes and thinking about what I would say, which altered my experience of the work, particularly, I think, when it was fiction. Reading and writing in quantity, on deadline, can be wearing, even deadening. In time, confronting a steady lineup of books, you are hard put not to feel that you're processing them: taking them in and grinding out responses in 750-word chunks. Responses can lose their spontaneity; the books begin to seem the same. Writing can easily become formulaic; the reviews begin to sound the same.

For the occasional reviewer, a reviewing assignment has status. Fiction writers or poets who review can think of themselves as following in the tradition of "men of letters," taking their place in the larger literary world. Teachers and lawyers who review are admired because they are teachers and lawyers who also review: somehow they find the time, admirably they have this additional ability. Occasional reviewers, who aren't particularly involved in the field, are probably not aware that reviewers have been called vermin or that they are considered failed writers. As the review editor Donald Davidson observed, remarking on his preference for amateur reviewers, they "have not yet learned the sad lesson that criticism is one of the most impermanent and least respected forms of writing."[13] Nor would the scorn, if they should be aware of it, necessarily matter: it applies to reviewers, and they don't see themselves essentially as reviewers, they're teachers or lawyers or librarians who review. Reviewing, for them, isn't evidence that they're failed writers; on the contrary, it's evidence that they are writers.

It's the professional reviewers, the writers who see themselves primarily as reviewers, who will suffer from the denigration of the field. They haven't another field that claims them; reviewing is their work, it's where their egos are invested. As a reviewer, I found it infuriating to hear people describe reviewing as easy, something anyone could do, or tell me that "they too review," because they'd posted a few reviews on Amazon. As someone who took reviewing seriously, I found it discouraging to hear literary people talk about reviewing as something you do before moving on to "bigger and more ambitious things." And I found it dispiriting when people would ask, as any reviewer will tell you they so often do, "Do you have work of your own?"

Nothing seems to me more revealing about our cultural attitude toward book reviewing than this question of having "work of one's own," which seems peculiarly related to this genre of critical journalism. We don't expect the financial journalist to be a banker or the political reporter to be a politician. I can't quite hear anyone asking Pauline Kael, John Simon, or Arlene Croce if they have work of their own, meaning do they make movies, write plays or music, or choreograph dance. We expect these critics to have a deep knowledge of their fields. And we view what they write— their commentary, their views, their philosophy and distinctive prose style—as their work, their own work. But book reviewers, perhaps because they're working in print, the same medium as the work they're critiquing, or perhaps because there are so many of them, find the very concept of a calling—or even a career—in reviewing dismissed.

Of course, arts critics in general have often been disparaged (particularly by artists they've criticized) for not being artists themselves, and therefore lacking the expertise, the experience, the talent, the very right to make judgments. In book reviewing, the reviewer is often implicitly compared—unfavorably—with the author.

"It is the lot of the critic . . . no matter how influential or how capably he eventually comes to terms with the real nature of his talent, to be regarded as someone who falls short," wrote the English critic Alan Ross, commenting in the *Times Literary Supplement* on Desmond MacCarthy, who, like Cyril Connolly, spent much of his career reviewing and was criticized for not doing "creative" work. "Neither in fact was remotely inventive or imaginative, but each managed to write better and more rewardingly than all but a handful of their contemporaries. Both were criticized for not having written less journalism, when journalism was not only their bread and butter but their vocation."[14]

Ross was writing about England, but the situation seems to me worse here, where we have had a weaker tradition of literary journalism. As the critic Dwight Garner once remarked, in an article on reviewing in America, "In today's literary culture, the authors of grindingly second-rate novels are far more revered than first-rate essayists."[15] This admiration is visible even on the reviewer's own turf, where he sees editors passing on some of the most prestigious assignments—the books that will get lead reviews—to novelists whose critical skills aren't notable, indeed, may not exist. Our worship of "creative writing," fiction writing in particular, fills our writing programs and brings admiration for the author of a published book, whether or not the work is any good. But first-rate reviewers are seen as lacking "creative" talent rather than as having a talent for reviewing, and if they bring their critical skills to bear too sharply, they're likely to be met with the accusation that they're frustrated novelists themselves, envious of the creative writers they review.

The conception of the reviewer taking revenge on "real" writers is long-standing and widespread. Connolly, who famously embraced the image, addressed it with bitter wit: "Every good reviewer has a subject. He specializes in that subject on which he has not been able to write a book, and his aim is to see that no one else does. He stands behind the ticket queue of fame, banging his rivals on the head as they bend low before the guichet. When he has laid out enough he becomes an authority, which is more than they will."[16]

In an article for the *Boston Globe,* the writer Michael Dorris also raised this specter of the failed writer sharpening her critical penknife. He conjured up an imaginary reviewer, "Elaine Zud," who, "for all we know," is a frustrated novelist whose "tattered manuscript . . . has been rejected by every publisher in New York," and who, "in her infinite wisdom and fairness . . . confronts each new book with a muttered, 'Ha! I can write rings around this hack!'"[17]

If the acidic ink of envy has been commonly seen as a weapon in the hands of vengeful failures, Charles Miner Thompson, writing a century ago in the *Atlantic Monthly,* held a different and, I think, more perceptive view of reviewers. He too believed that critics were generally "disappointed authors," but in his view this did not necessarily mean they were incompetent to judge or blinded by jealousy. Dismissing the theory that we are incompetent to judge a task which we cannot perform—as "no writer ever refrained out of deference to it from criticising, or even discharging, his cook"—he argued that

> jealousy does not always blind, sometimes it gives keenness of vision. The disappointed author turned critic may indeed be incompetent; but, if he is so, it is for reasons that his disappointment does not supply. If he is able, his disappointment will, on the contrary, help his criticism. He will have a wholesome contempt for facile success; he will measure by exacting standards. Moreover, the thoughts of a talented man about an art for the attainment of which he has striven to the point of despair are certain to be valuable; his study of the masters has been intense, his study of his contemporaries has had the keenness of an ambitious search for the key to success.[18]

What seems to me most interesting about this widespread conception of reviewer envy and spiteful revenge is the unquestioning acceptance that it's common. As it happens, praise rather than nastiness has generally been the central problem in American reviewing, and it is hard to reconcile the image of "disappointed authors" intent on ripping apart their successful rivals with the lavish encomiums that they've been heaping on books for years, as critics of reviewing have long complained, and which we see on our book pages weekly. It seems more likely that in a culture that thinks little of reviewing and highly of book writing, we have projected this envy on reviewers, unable to comprehend that they might have a talent for reviewing and want to use it, that they might actually enjoy reviewing and see it as a vocation.

Whatever the truth of reviewer-envy or lack of it, the belief in it is yet another factor that makes it hard for serious reviewers to do good work. Wary of being viewed as jealous, reviewers shy away from pointed criticism, bending over backward to praise books more than they deserve. Fearful of being considered enviously unfair, they lay out so many compliments—to prove their goodwill—that when they finally reach their criticism, which is offered with an apologetic bow, they end up sounding foolish. Unwilling to be viewed as failed writers, they overwrite: "Autobiography is a cruel genre, asking as it does that the finitudes of history be colored with the timeless hues of art,"[19] says the reviewer, who sounds to me overeager to prove that she is a "real" writer too.

Reviewers have good reason to be disappointed, not as authors but as reviewers, who are faced, in the workplace, with a series of double binds. The reviewer's work is demanding, but its lowly fee implies that it has little value. Like novelists and poets, reviewers seem to be expected to work for the love of writing; yet they're denied the status of writers with work of their own. Because there is so little recognition of the difficulty of reviewing, there is little appreciation of the intelligence, skill, and time a good piece of criticism requires; and since the difficulty isn't acknowledged, everyone is quick to gripe when the job—which isn't hard, after all—is badly done. Instead of countering these perceptions, editorial practices in the field appear to support them. By failing to ask reviewers for resumes or summaries of their reading, review editors imply that little education or reading knowledge is needed for the job, that whatever qualifications they have will "do." By turning to authors for reviews simply because they are authors—and handing them lead assignments if they're sufficiently celebrated—editors suggest that even on the book page, critical skills play second fiddle to "creative" skills and reaffirm reviewers' lesser status. By publishing uncritical, illogical, or overwritten reviews, editors fail to encourage or teach reviewers to do good work; still worse, they suggest that it doesn't really matter.

As far as ever from Sherman's hope of developing or rewarding a professional literary class, our book-reviewing practices seem designed, on the one hand, to drive many of those with critical talent into academia, where they can receive not only appreciation and even acclaim but a job and, no small thing, a salary, and, on the other, to foil those who remain in the field because they love the work and want to undertake it in earnest, perversely discouraging the very people we most need.

The Match

...a tasteless exercise ... an ego trip disguised as a novel.

—Paul Erdman on Michael Thomas's novel *Hard Money*

It fails miserably (and) ... left me with a nasty taste.

—Michael Thomas on Paul Erdman's novel *The Last Days of America*
(Cross-reviews cited by David Shaw, *Los Angeles Times,* 1985)

Sir,—I have not yet seen *1798: The year of the Lyrical Ballads.* This book was
so warmly reviewed by Seamus Perry ... that I look forward to reading it.
At the same time, I must observe that Nicola Trott ("an accomplished, nim-
ble piece") is Dr Perry's wife; the editor, Richard Cronin ("deftly reads
Gebir"), is Perry's head of department; and Dorothy McMillan ("finds in
Joanna Baillie a quasi-scientific project") is Mr Cronin's wife. All are in the
Department of English Literature at Glasgow University, as are several oth-
er contributors to the volume (and as I was myself, until fairly recently).

I do not blame Dr Perry for being fond of his colleagues, nor do I doubt
the efficacy of their contributions to knowledge. But a degree of disinterest
in literary criticism is always welcome.

—Letters to the Editor, *TLS,* October 9, 1998

Most of the thousands of poets were bad, most of the thousands of critics
were bad, and they loved each other.

—Randall Jarrell, Letter to the *Nation,* 1948

*I*f the first-time author worries most about whether her book will be
reviewed, the author publishing his fifth worries equally about who

will review it: authors learn, sometimes painfully, just how much the assignment matters. In my own worst-case scenario, this book on reviewing is assigned to one of the reviewers I've criticized—perhaps the one I called sophomoric, or the one I said was incoherent—who proceeds to take his or her revenge.

No aspect of reviewing is more charged than the matchup of books and reviewers: the choice of reviewer inevitably determines the outcome of the review. This is the case even if the editor is neutral in his search for a critic. Every reader has his own response to a book; different reviewers will write different reviews: John Reviewer may love the novel's "lyricism," while Jane Reviewer loathes its "pretentious imagery"; Jane may find the memoir's nonlinear narrative "original and arresting," while John finds it "fragmented and confusing"; one New York reviewer pans novel X for mismapping Manhattan, another finds the book's errors irrelevant in a "terrific read," and a Chicago reviewer, who doesn't know the Lower East Side from the Upper West, praises the author's use of locale. The author is lucky or not. And of course if an editor isn't neutral, if he seeks out a particular viewpoint or goes with a reviewer who has one, his choice will not only determine the outcome of the review but may predetermine it as well.

In an ideal world, every reviewer assigned to a book would be appropriately knowledgeable to deal with it, sufficiently sympathetic to be able to respond to it, and unbiased for or against. In the real world, the matchup makes for some dubious bedfellows: In the *New York Times Book Review,* I find a book by *Times* columnist Maureen Dowd reviewed by Kathryn Harrison—whose memoir Dowd had once described, none too kindly, as "creepy people talking about creepy people." (Not a rave review.) In an issue of the *New York Observer,* Robert Gottlieb reviews a memoir by a former colleague, whose memories of Gottlieb, the reviewer tells us, are "warm and generous." (He found the book a "triumph.") In the *Washington Post Book World,* an anticonservative memoir is reviewed by a well-known conservative who, it turns out, is mentioned in the book (which he panned). And in the *New York Times Book Review,* a book critical of the *New York Times* is reviewed by a reporter who, as it happens, is a member of the *Times*'s own Washington Bureau. (Not a favorable review.)[1]

Most curiously, in the *New York Times Book Review,* a reviewer, writing about a mystery, pauses midstream to tell readers that he neither likes nor pays much attention to the genre. "Let me confess that I am not a great reader of thrillers or detective fiction," he declares, apparently unconcerned that this might make him a mystery reviewer of questionable value. "The latter in particular, it seems to me, lies under the tyranny of procedure—the scene of the crime, the autopsy, the interviews, the suspects, the false accusations—all of which can make such stories as weirdly stylized as Kabuki theater."[2] Having praised the book for the degree to which it isn't merely a mystery—indeed, does not, in his opinion, really succeed as a mystery—he concludes with that shopworn praise about the book transcending the genre, leaving us to wonder why someone with such a low opinion of—and apparently little engagement with—mysteries had been asked, and had agreed, to review one.

Whether a marriage of passion or convenience, a bond forged by chance or for gain, the critical matchup, like any marriage, is both a public and a private affair: subject to circumstance, temptation, and a slew of constraints.

For editors, as for authors, the matchup is chancy. The editor doesn't write the review; he only picks the reviewer, about whom he often knows only what the reviewer chooses to reveal. The reviewer may fail to let him know he isn't fully qualified to assess the book, that he dislikes the particular genre, or that the author is the head of his English department, his poker partner, his lover's ex, or the villain who trashed his own last novel.

Every book makes it own demands. The editor needs to consider subject expertise and competence. He needs to consider sympathies and temperament. He needs to consider status. For the book by a celebrated author, if he wants an honest review, he'll need a reviewer confident enough to be unintimidated: this is not the time to call upon a novice. For the first novel, if he wants a kind review, he'll need a forgiving reviewer: this is not the time to call upon his most acerbic critic. For the book by a powerful author, he'll need to find a reviewer who has nothing to lose: as books editor of the *Radcliffe Quarterly,* an alumnae magazine that was hardly a hotbed of vitriolic commentary, I had to ask four reviewers before I found one willing to take on a book by Helen Vendler, the grande dame of poetry criticism.

Editors bring their own demands. However much they may strive for neutrality, they can't be uninvolved. The matches determine the character and quality of the book page, and whatever they want for that book page, this is their chance to make it happen. For editors, this is an exciting part of the job, a creative part of the process, their contribution to the review. No sooner does a book come into play than names of potential reviewers are danced around: different reviews shaped by different hands are considered. Sometimes it's the intriguing match that determines the selection of a title or the absence of the right reviewer that leads the editor to ignore it. And editors, of course, aren't always neutral. They may have no views one way or the other about a book on Arctic exploration or a biography of W. C. Fields, but they'll probably have strong opinions about America's best-known writers, current literary trends, and social issues, and they may have a hard time suppressing them. They may not even try.

And publications have their impact. Partisan publications want partisan viewpoints: magazines on the left or right will alienate readers—and lose subscriptions—by praising the opposition's books: Readers don't always want "objective" reviews. For prestigious periodicals and books, the enterprise is competitive—editors speak of "wooing" and "snaring" reviewers—and the playing field isn't level. Some publications can offer reviewers a larger or more desirable circulation, higher fees, more space. Editors of smaller, less well-endowed publications have to rely upon ingenuity in luring reviewers or speed in getting to them first. As Paul Baumann, executive editor of *Commonweal* magazine, once observed: "Snatching a reviewer from the grasp of bigger and far wealthier competitors is a bit like going dateless to the prom and coming home with the prom queen."[3]

As suitors and go-betweens, employers and supplicants, editors will find themselves juggling conflicting aims, and even the most scrupulous will be forced to make trade-offs. Some of these will be minor. But as many matchups make clear, too often editors barter badly, miscalculate costs, and neglect to ask the prom queen what books—or authors—she takes to bed.

The most basic question assigning editors face, it seems to me, is competence: deciding just what kind a book needs. Some books are so clearly specialized that editors know they have to find a reviewer with appropriate expertise. But most books, even if they're written for the general reader, require some background knowledge. Popular works may demand less knowledge of readers, but I think it's debatable whether the demand on reviewers really differs. On what basis can a reviewer evaluate even a popular biography of Woodrow Wilson unless she has a solid knowledge of the history? If she is a reader of biography, she can evaluate it within the genre, but it's a pretty limited assessment if she finds it a "wonderfully written life" and misses the fact that much of it is inaccurate. On what basis can a reviewer assess a travel book set in Austria if she has never been there? She can evaluate the work as literature but will be unable to judge its validity. For all the reviewer knows, the book's descriptions, however vivid, may be untrue.

The publisher Henry Holt credited the *Nation* back in the 1860s for the practice of matching books with knowledgeable reviewers as a matter of policy. In his 1923 memoir, *Garrulities of an Octogenarian Editor,* Holt describes—with appropriate garrulity—a visit from the *Nation*'s John Dennett:

> I still vividly remember my surprise and enlightenment when Dennett happened into my office just as the first volume of Taine's *Italy* came in from the binder, and I handed him a copy, and he said: "Let me see! To whom shall I send this for review—who knows Italy?" And after a little reflection he decided to send it to Howells. Now, so far as I know, doing this as a matter of course was something new in American journalism. It must have been done exceptionally and spasmodically by two or three of the heavier periodicals, such as the *North American* and the *Atlantic,* but the general habit was to turn everything over to a "book reviewer"—a "literary gentleman," such as one newspaper about that time complacently assured the publishing world, by circular, it had added to its staff. This novel course by the *Nation* gave it an authority looked upon by those as ignorant as I was, with almost superstitious awe, and it was a very short time before its favorable verdict was accepted by everybody as final; and also its unfavorable verdict, by everybody but the interested parties.[4]

Nowadays we might question the editorial ethics of Mr. Dennett wandering around a publisher's office. But there's no question that in terms of expertise Howells was a good match for Taine's book—he really did "know" Italy: he published his own book, *Italian Journeys,* in 1867. Nor is there any question that most editors want knowledgeable matches, which, as Holt observed, provide authority. In his lively description of editorial matchmaking, "Confessions of a Book Review Editor," *Commonweal*'s Paul Baumann describes finding just the right reviewer for James Carroll's *Constantine's Sword: The Church and the Jews, a History,* a historian who could—and did—address "exactly the point the mainstream reviews would miss."[5]

But in general, editors will have a hard time finding such reviewers for every title they deal with. They need to identify appropriate reviewers, locate them, contact them, discuss the projects, and persuade them to take them on. Most editors haven't the resources necessary to do all this for every book. They're generally working without staff, money, or time. While the *New York Times Book Review,* which has made a point of trying to match books with qualified reviewers, has a deep list of critics from various fields who have previously expressed interest in reviewing for them or have reviewed for them before, few editors have that kind of access or the ability to lure such reviewers. Not all experts will be willing to write a five-hundred-word review for *Small Town Daily* for a fee of fifty dollars.

Moreover, these specialists, should they be found and hired, don't necessarily make good reviewers. It's one thing to find a William Dean Howells, who was a writer, critic, and editor. Nowadays, most of the people who are ideally qualified in terms of subject expertise and breadth of reading, in fiction as well as nonfiction, are likely to be academics, accustomed to academic writing and discourse—and as someone who has edited such writers, I know well the problems they present. In their own spheres they'll have had no need to make their points accessible to a general audience and will have had little practice in translating what they have to say into readable, let alone lively, entertaining prose. On the contrary, the jargon-fraught texts of academia suggest that inaccessibility may be a goal, a mark of intellectual validity: the less comprehensible the better. Absorbed in the finer points of their specialized viewpoints, they may have little sense of what constitutes a general-interest review. Rather than addressing issues of broad concern that are of interest to nonspecialist readers, they may skew their critiques too narrowly, picking on points that matter little to people outside their own fields. Academic reviewers are also likely to be partisan, to belong to one school or another. If they've written on the subject under review—which is probably how the editor identified them in the first place—they'll have a viewpoint to defend and may use their review to defend it.

From a practical standpoint, general-interest editors may have a hard time working with reviewers who are used to scholarly ways, especially scholarly time frames: academic reviews are notoriously late. Writing in *Publishers Weekly,* one editor of an academic journal, Stanley B. Winters, lamented that in his experience, "the normal three-month deadline for a 400- to 500-word review meant nothing. Most reviewers took six to eight months, sometimes a year. Canadian and European reviewers were generally more punctual than Americans, with the exception of a few Austrians and Germans to whom time seemed meaningless."[6] The "record for tardiness" on his watch was set by an American professor, who managed to take five years.

Editors of academic journals encounter these scenarios routinely; however much they may yearn for timely, fair reviews written in good English, they have to put up with the jargon, bias, and lateness that often accompany expertise: uninformed reviews will put them out of business. But for general-interest editors, the reverse is the case; however much they may hope for informed reviews, they will have to put up with the lack of expertise that characterizes the general-interest review: unreadable reviews will put them out of business.

Between the difficulty of finding specialists and the problems posed by their work, editors have come to rely more heavily on generalists. But among the generalists, each one usually has a "specialty." Most editors rely upon a group of trusted reviewers—a "stable," as it's usually referred to—to come through with decently written reviews that meet word length and deadlines in the areas they cover. These areas of interest are broad—fiction, biography, history—and often the reviewers have qualified by reading preferences rather than by training, which can result in the appearance of specialization without much depth of knowledge. The political columnist to whom the review editor routinely turns for coverage of presidential biographies, for example, may have a solid background in history or a superficial one; political columnists are not historians. The fiction writer or fiction lover the review editor regularly hires to review novels may or may not have the breadth of reading, past or present, that would give depth to her criticism.

In their search for nonspecialist writers with links to certain topics, editors come up with connections that go beyond superficial to artificial. The Indian writer is asked to review Indian literature. The author of a memoir is asked to review biographies. A novelist who happens to be a working mother is asked to review a nonfiction book on working mothers. As a first-fiction columnist, I was asked to review, along with first novels, the first English translations of fiction by foreign authors: one artificial category extending to another.

The reviewing community has long had faith in the generalists who have historically formed the bulk of our reviewing workforce. As American book reviewing expanded in the twentieth century, newspapers and magazines came to rely upon staff reviewers who wrote about a wide range of books, much as today the daily *New York Times* reviewers, the columnists at the *Washington Post Book World,* and review editors at other papers and magazines still do. This belief in the generalist reviewer differs from the belief we find on bookselling and review sites on the Web, the democratic idea that every reader has something of value to offer. The review editor's faith is based on the idea that an intelligent, widely read, responsive reviewer who can write with wit will have something of value to say about books even if he's not knowledgeable about the subject. Editors sometimes urge reviewers whose work they like to take on a wider range of topics, counting on their expertise as readers and reviewers to turn in a creditable critique and hoping their fresh perspective will add interest. One of my worst reviews—of Barbara Tuchman's *The First Salute,* a book entirely outside my field—was a response to such a request, and, to my regret, it seems alive still in blurbs on the Web.

This faith in the generalist wouldn't be misplaced if it were predicated on reviewers' having done the appropriate background reading and research for a specific book. A reviewer can't become an instant expert, but he can bring an intelligent, informed perspective to a book if he has read, say, all the author's previous work, several other biographies of the figure whose latest biography he's reviewing, various travel accounts of whatever country is the subject of his review. But in my experience, review editors don't require this. No editor has ever suggested doing background reading or inquired whether I've done it. Indeed, in one of my more bizarre experiences as a freelance reviewer, I agreed to review a book about Henry James for a respectable literary magazine only to find, when the book arrived, that in fact it was about Henry's brother William. In a note tucked into the volume, the assigning editor apologized for the error and seemed to hope that it wouldn't make a difference. If it seems ludicrous to assume that a reviewer qualified to write about the novelist would automatically be qualified to write about the psychologist, it's worth noting that since he hadn't asked about my background in the first place, he had no idea whether I was qualified for either.

Editors may well feel it would be inappropriate—even outrageous—to demand background reading when they're paying so little. The typical fee fails to adequately cover the time spent reading and reviewing one book let alone the time required to track down ten out-of-print titles in various libraries and read them. Nor, within the typical time frame, can they provide even those reviewers who are willing to do the work with the weeks necessary to do it. But without this background reading, reviews tend to be not only uninformed and unsophisticated but also timid; reviewers who know that they don't really know enough to evaluate what they're reading are reluctant to be critical and instead are far more likely to be mildly praising or noncommittal. They will also lack the contextual knowledge necessary to fully engage with the book, and the editor who avoided the expert in the hope of getting an interesting review often ends up with something decently written but bland.

Obviously, editors don't want bland reviews: dullness is the enemy of the book page. Few enough Americans are interested in reading about books, and boring reviews will drive even those few away. What editors hope in assigning a book is that something will be sparked in the matchup, that the reviewer will respond to the book. It is the response, positive or negative, that animates reviewer and review. Editors, having selected a book, run through their list of potential reviewers trying to find the right person. They judge by the reviewers' known interests, their responses to previous books, or just an editorial intuition that reviewer and book will hit it off. Some editors have a talent for the process, a nose for the likely match as well as the imaginative, apparently improbable, pairing that will elicit a provocative review.

But taste is individual, and unpredictable. As George Orwell observed, "Nearly every book is capable of arousing passionate feeling, if it is only a passionate dislike, in some or other reader."[7] But as he also noted, finding that reader will be difficult. One of the virtues of the reviewers on bookselling and personal Web sites is that they're a self-selected group of such critics, commenting on books—or films, or classical or popular music—to which they've responded strongly and about which they feel they have something to say. By contrast, traditional book reviewers are passive recipients of works their editors have chosen. Even if the editor has read and liked the book, there is no guarantee the reviewer will agree. And in general, editors have done neither and only sent it along hoping the reviewer might find it of interest.

Serendipity can occur. All reviewers are familiar with the experience of receiving wonderful books they might not otherwise have read, which is one of the rewards of reviewing. But the books most likely to elicit a response in a reviewer, as in the majority of readers, usually do so because they're exceptionally good or exceptionally bad, and most books sent out for review are mediocre. This is the case because, although we may hate to admit it, most books *are* mediocre, and the traditional methods of selecting books—by author, subject, publisher, publicity—don't screen out mediocrity. All reviewers are also familiar with the experience of taking on forgettable books and facing the insuperable task of trying to find something noteworthy to say about them. No one has evoked this situation better than Orwell, who himself reviewed extensively and wrote about it with knowing humor:

> A periodical gets its weekly wad of books and sends off a dozen of them to X, the hack reviewer . . . To begin with, the chances are that eleven out of the twelve books will fail to rouse in him the faintest spark of interest. They are not more than ordinarily bad, they are merely neutral, lifeless and pointless. If he were not paid to do so he would never read a line of any of them, and in nearly every case the only truthful review he could write would be: "This book inspires in me no thoughts whatever." But will anyone pay you to write that kind of thing? Obviously not. As a start, therefore, X is in the false position of having to manufacture, say, three hundred words about a book which means nothing to him whatever. Usually he does it by giving a brief resume of the plot (incidentally betraying to the author the fact that he hasn't read the book) and handing out a few compliments which for all their fulsomeness are about as valuable as the smile of a prostitute.[8]

To avoid such "manufactured responses," which are not only dishonest but also boring to read, editors sometimes forfeit disinterest and seek out a reviewer they know beforehand will respond strongly to a book: a reviewer who has previously written on the subject and is known to loathe or love an author's work, a particular style of writing, or a genre; a reviewer whose work—or who himself—figures in the book under review. What editors gain when they select this way are critics already in possession of articulated viewpoints and arguments, critics so engaged by the issues raised by books that they can work up their passion even if the works themselves are mediocre.

But the downside of such matchups is self-evident. All too often the passionate reviewer who approaches a book with a viewpoint just "happens" to find that viewpoint confirmed: the critic who loathes postmodern fiction finds that John Barth's new novel is lamentably bad; the critic who believes that science fiction isn't "real" literature finds that Margaret Atwood's new science fiction novel proves the point; the political scientist who has argued in his own book that affirmative action doesn't work concludes that a new book on the subject fails to show that it does. Unlike reviewers who have to simulate opinions, these critics have genuine opinions; the trouble is, they aren't necessarily responses to the books at hand. Too often these partisan reviewers could have written the reviews before they read the books.

As a way to elicit interesting reviews, such setups seem to me self-defeating. At best, they can lead to lively essays, provided the reviewer, who has this material in stock, hasn't used it so often that it's been worn thin by recycling: an essay on the failings of postmodern fiction, the literary limitations of science fiction, the problems of affirmative action can certainly be interesting. But for a review to be provocative as a review, we need a critic responding to a particular book: the review is the story of that response, and it proves a dull tale for reviewers and readers if it holds no element of surprise. And of course such setups are seldom fair.

It's the pervasive potential for unfairness that makes the matchup so charged. The search for a qualified reviewer can easily lead to a biased critic. The search for a responsive reviewer can easily lead to a biased critic. The search for a provocative review can easily lead to a biased critic. And if an editor has strong views, he may find it hard to resist finding a biased critic who supports them. The ethic of resistance in the field is weak. In general I've found there's disapproval of an editor deliberately seeking an unfavorable review but approval of the opposite, though it's questionable whether it's really more fair to seek out a positive than a negative opinion. And some editors feel comfortable seeking either. In a three-part series on book reviewing that David Shaw wrote for the *Los Angeles Times* in 1985, John Leonard told the reporter that as editor of the *New York Times Book Review*, "I was inclined—always, every single time—to send a book to someone who shared my judgment . . . , if I had one . . . I remember finding one book hateful and obnoxious, and I was going to ignore it, but one writer I was talking to said he hated it, too, so I gave it to him and he killed it."[9]

It isn't only authors who don't get a fair chance in such cases. Readers often have no way of knowing that a match has been unfair and that a book hasn't stood or fallen on its own. Occasionally, when matchups are particularly egregious, the press will take note; from time to time *Columbia Journalism Review*, a publication that monitors the press, will devote a "dart" in its "Darts and Laurels" column to a lapse in book-reviewing ethics. The column gave a dart to the *Tulsa World* and its book editor, who revealed, in the last sentence of his review of a book he said was "destined to become a classic," that he himself was its author. (At least Anthony Burgess, when he reviewed his own book under a pseudonym, had the grace to mock it: he called the book a "laughing-stock.") "Darts and Laurels" certainly paid attention when the *Washington Post*, the *New York Times Book Review*, and the *Wall Street Journal*, all of which were criticized in *The Hunting of the President* for their coverage of Bill Clinton, all assigned the book to reviewers they could count on to pan it. Sometimes, within reviews, a critic will acknowledge his relationship to book or author, as Robert Gottlieb did in his *New York Observer* review of a book in which he played a role. Such disclosure at least lets readers know where the reviewer is coming from, though the commentary is still hardly disinterested and in some cases really should be called a "response" to the book rather than a "review." More appropriately, when—again in the *New York Observer*—Gottlieb, a former editor of the *New Yorker*, discussed a book about the *New Yorker* in which he acknowledged that he turned up as "one of the bad guys," the publication ran the long negative piece as an "Observatory" article and didn't call it a "book review."[10]

Most often, though, readers learn about unfair matches in letters to the editor, generally from authors and their friends when books are trashed and from rivals when they're praised. These letters often smack so strongly of partisanship or, if they're written by authors, sour grapes, that it's easy to dismiss them. And yet they offer readers otherwise-unavailable insight into the matching process.

In one of book reviewing's more highly publicized brouhahas, back in 1991, Norman Mailer wrote a full-page letter to the *New York Times Book Review* protesting the editor's choice of John Simon as reviewer for his novel *Harlot's Ghost*. Writing with his typical flair for high drama, and referring to himself in the third person, of course, Mailer turned the episode into something of a show—especially since he had very little to say about the review, only the reviewer. Nonetheless, Mailer made his case.

Contending that Simon was not a fair choice as reviewer because he had shown himself in the past to be anything but neutral about Mailer's work, the author cited Simon's review of *The Armies of the Night*, which the critic had called "almost unrelieved self-promotion, often in atrocious prose . . . a demented Waring blender churning away at sexual, political, and literary power fantasies, sadomasochistic day-dreams." Still worse, though it would hardly seem possible, Simon had called Mailer's *Marilyn* ". . . a labor of lust . . . a new genre called transcendental masturbation or metaphysical wet dreaming . . . a grisly roller-coaster ride along a biceps gone berserk . . ." Mailer, said Simon,

> needs neither sex nor food to be nauseating; he can do it with mere hyperbole . . . *Marilyn* is a very poorly written, very demented book, by someone whom our deluded critics persist in treating as a major, perhaps our best, writer. And it won't do to say that Mailer has only lately gone around the bend: there is less than a Chappaquiddick wheel's deviation between these onanistic lucubrations on the late sex star, the nude and deceased, and that supposedly brilliant first novel on the naked and the dead.[11]

Not a Mailer fan, we would probably agree. Although, as it turned out, Mailer found Simon's review of *Harlot's Ghost* "curiously spineless," lacking in the critic's "vintage bile," he was surely right in judging Simon an inappropriate choice. It's hard to see how an editor seeking a fair reviewer—if she had read that review of *Marilyn,* as the *Times Book Review* editor Rebecca Sinkler said she had—would turn to someone who so disliked even the work considered Mailer's best. It would seem obvious that he would probably dislike anything Mailer wrote and might well have used the review to prove that the critics who thought him a major writer were wrong.

But most mismatches don't receive the publicity generated by the Mailer-Simon episode, which gave rise to a lively batch of reader correspondence as well as coverage in other publications. Authors who feel their work has been unfairly assigned aren't generally offered the space for a full-page reply nor are they granted, as Mailer was, a response not only from the reviewer but from the editor as well. And few authors are as little likely to be damaged by a mismatch as Mailer, who has both literary status and the nerve to fight back. Most letters of complaint from authors are mocked, which is why writers are usually urged—by editors, agents, and friends—not to send them. Authors have no viable remedy when they feel they've been wronged.

With so much riding on the choice of reviewer, both for readers and authors, and so little discussion of the issues in the field, I was glad to see the National Book Critics Circle focus attention on the topic in two ethics surveys it distributed to members, one in 1988 and another in 2001. Although the latter had too few responses to be significant, the earlier one was revealing. Twenty out of the twenty-nine questions focused on matchups with their enormous potential for conflicts of interest. These included such expected questions as whether it's acceptable for an editor to assign a book to a friend or even an acquaintance of the author. But the survey also ranged further afield. Should an editor assign a book to a reviewer who has written a book on the same subject as the author, or to a reviewer who has written such a book that hasn't yet been published? Should she assign a book to a reviewer who shares a publisher or literary agent with the author, who has blurbed a book, who is mentioned in the acknowledgments or recommended by the publisher?

If the number and range of questions suggested the many ways that bias can creep into a review, the diversity of answers made it clear that the reviewing community held very different opinions about what might unfairly influence reviewers' judgments—or at any rate their reviews—of a book. Indeed, the president of the National Book Critics Circle observed that although she had hoped the survey might be "the starting point for an NBCC 'code' of reviewing ethics," such hopes were dashed by the level of disagreement the answers revealed.[12]

To some degree the disparity in the answers—and the questionnaire itself—illuminated just how ambiguous many reviewing situations are. After all, if it's wrong to assign a book to a reviewer "who is known to hold aesthetic, political or literary principles contrary to those of the author" and also wrong to assign a book to a reviewer "who is known to hold aesthetic, political or literary views similar to the author's," the poor editor in many cases will be left with reviewers who have no critical intelligence at all.[13]

But the answers also pointed to some of the problems evident in the choices editors and reviewers make. While 82 of 124 of the respondents said that anyone mentioned in the acknowledgments of a book should be barred from reviewing it, 37 respondents, almost 30 percent, said they needn't be. While almost 40 percent said that a review shouldn't be assigned to someone who had written a book on the same subject which would not "be released until sometime in the future," a majority, over 56 percent, approved of such a match. And while more than 82 percent said that it was unacceptable to assign a book to a friend of the author, over 86 percent felt it was acceptable to assign it to a "casual acquaintance."

But is it really plausible that someone mentioned in the acknowledgments of a book would be sufficiently objective to review it? At the least, if the acknowledgment was token, they would feel they'd been accorded respect; if they'd helped with the book, either they would feel they'd participated in making it better or, if their advice had been ignored, they might feel annoyed. But surely they would feel something about the book and probably about the author. And how could any reviewer be objective about a book on the same subject as one he had written which was preceding his into the field? Even if he avoided the temptation to pan it in the hope of saving room on the bookshelves for his own, it's hard to imagine his failing to compare the two, reviewing one with the other perhaps nervously, perhaps arrogantly, in mind.

As for "casual acquaintances," the term can take in a great variety of relationships, from meeting someone at a party to serving together on a panel, but I find it improbable that the personal element would have no impact on a review, that the friendly or obnoxious encounter wouldn't be somewhere in the reviewer's mind, influencing what she found herself willing to say. Perhaps I'm more susceptible than other reviewers, but I find that I generally form impressions, whether positive or negative, about people, and I wouldn't trust myself to keep their influence entirely out of a review. Only once did I review the book of anyone with whom I was even remotely acquainted—and this was exceedingly remote—and though I didn't like the book, I also didn't like the author, and I have always wondered whether the two were as separate as I would like to believe. In England, it's apparently common practice to assign reviews even to friends, in part, suggests Victoria Glendinning, because the circle of writers and reviewers is smaller than it is in the United States, and when someone who is part of that circle "opens his Sunday paper . . . he will know personally most of the people whose names head the reviews. And when his own next book comes to be reviewed his assassin, if the notice is murderous, is likely to be an acquaintance, if not, any longer, a friend."[14] But that "casualness" about reviewer relationships may be part of the reason English reviews are far more likely than ours to be murderous.

Surveys and statistics have their limitations, but if these answers reflect a way of thinking, it seems to me that editors and reviewers often leave themselves open to matches in which unwanted and unacknowledged factors are bound to play a role in shaping what gets said. In practice, the situation is made worse by the fact that most publications lack a formal written ethics policy, and few editors query reviewers about their relationships to the authors or books under review. In his series on reviewing, which was based on more than one hundred interviews with reviewers, editors, and others in the reviewing and publishing community, David Shaw observed that while editors at major papers say they try to ask about relationships, "many reviewers interviewed for this story said they've never been asked about possible conflicts by any editors."[15] Writing in the National Book Critics Circle journal in 1993, Steve Weinberg observed that in seventeen years of extensive reviewing—he noted more than five hundred reviews for about thirty publications—"not once" had an assigning editor asked him about conflicts of interest. Moreover, he said, in those seventeen years, he had seen only one written policy, which he discovered not in the course of reviewing but while he was doing research on the sub-ject for an article.[16] My own experience bears this out. Apart from one ex-tremely careful editor, who wouldn't even send me books by authors who lived in my city, I was never asked about my relationship to authors or books. Nor, as an assigning editor, did I ask or have a written ethics poli-cy that would do the asking for me.

A basic ethics policy is such an easy thing to write—it need only be done once—that its general absence can only be explained by custom, a norm that is sustained by inertia. Editors' failure to ask about conflicts of inter-est is a more complex problem. The element of rush may play a role: in the discussion surrounding the details of the assignment, the question falls by the wayside. And checking on such conflicts is an awkward busi-ness in a relationship that is often unequal and dependent on goodwill: if editors are wooing reviewers, or even if they are simply friendly with them, they may not feel disposed to ask questions that sound accusatory and to risk alienating or even losing them. And because most publications have no policy, it isn't clear where the responsibility lies, whether editors should ask or reviewers should tell. It may be that each group is leaving it to the other to raise the issues, and in the end no one does. But most centrally, and this was certainly the case for me, the ethical dimension is simply too seldom on anyone's mind.

Writing about his experience as book editor of the *Philadelphia Inquir-er,* Larry Swindell once observed that at the start, he "accepted as gospel" what he had heard, that book selection was an editor's most important re-sponsibility, but in time he came to feel that it was

> more important that the book be given to the *right* reviewer. There is
> no particular honor in having a review of a high-profile book just for
> the record, if the review is misguided and misguiding for having been
> misassigned. When a book is reviewed by someone unqualified to
> judge it, or otherwise an injudicious choice for doing so, there is all-
> around disservice—to the author, to the publishers, to the readers of
> the review, and also to the reviewer himself.[17]

For such a pivotal aspect of reviewing, the matchup often receives re-markably casual treatment. Though it is inevitably chancy, open to error and bad faith, many editors don't take even the most minimal steps to di-minish the guesswork and increase the chances that reviews will be impartial and informed. In a field where David Shaw could find an editor asking a writer to review mysteries because her previous book had "crimes" in the title (though the book "had nothing to do with crime"),[18] where an editor can assign a book to a prominent critic who is thanked in the acknowledgments for help with that book's notes, where an editor can assign a book about Henry James and then blithely send the reviewer one about brother William, reviews are bound to be misguided, and "all-around disservice" in ample supply.

Getting It Right

mr highet: *the recognitions* was published in 1955, not 1954. mr hartman & kirkus service: it has 956 pages, not 965 or 946 mr demarest: it cost $7.50 hardcover, not $5.00 mr north: it was published by Harcourt, Brace—not Harcourt, Bruce mr yeiser: a chapter appeared in *New World Writing,* not *New Writing* livingston & north: characters in it are named Feasley, Feddle, Valentine—not Feasly, Feedle, Valentino mr o'hearn: the book is called *The Recognitions,* not *The Perceptions* mr dolbier: it was written by William Gaddis, not William Gibson

—Jack Green, recounting the errors in reviews of William Gaddis's *The Recognitions, Fire the Bastards!*

I proclaim to all the inhabitants of the land that they cannot trust to what the periodicals say of new books. Instead of being able by reading the criticism to judge of the book, it is now necessary to read the book in order to judge of the criticism.

—*Putnam's Monthly,* April 1855

In 1994, the publishing community—its reviewing contingent in particular—watched uneasily as a libel case came to court. The plaintiff was Dan Moldea, an investigative journalist, and the defendant was the *New York Times.* Moldea charged that the review of his book *Interference: How Organized Crime Influences Professional Football,* which had appeared in the *New York Times Book Review* on September 3, 1989, had tarnished his reputation as a crime reporter and damaged his career.

In his assessment of the book, the reviewer, Gerald Eskenazi, a *Times* sportswriter, had said that while the author raised "truly disturbing questions," there was "too much sloppy journalism to trust the bulk of this book's 512 pages—including its whopping 64 pages of notes." Eskenazi said that the author's "naivete is apparent, as is his ignorance of basic sports knowledge, while several errors in spelling call into question his diligence at simple fact-checking." And he concluded that in *Interference*, "with its errors and unfounded insinuations," Mr. Moldea had "blunted his own sword of truth."[1]

The review was decidedly negative, though modest on a scale of nastiness. But for Moldea, the issue was not that the review was negative but that it was inaccurate. As he told media critic Edwin Diamond in *New York Magazine*, "This is about an opinion that was based on a series of provably false facts."[2] Eskenazi, for example, had written that Moldea "revives the discredited notion that Carroll Rosenbloom, the ornery owner of the Rams, who had a penchant for gambling, met foul play when he drowned in Florida 10 years ago."[3] But Moldea pointed out that in the book he had written: "Rosenbloom died in a tragic accident and was not murdered." According to Moldea, the *New York Times Book Review* would neither print a correction of the errors in the review nor allow him space to respond. Claiming that the review had cost him his agent, his publisher, and potential writing contracts, he took his case to court, suing for ten million dollars.[4]

Historically, the courts have seldom been called upon to resolve disputes about fairness in reviewing, which, with other forms of criticism, has been protected by the First Amendment. Whatever a reviewer's judgment of a book, that judgment has been considered his opinion and, as opinion, not subject to legal action. Reviewers have at times been savage in their critiques. Frank Leslie's *Illustrated Newspaper,* reviewing Walt Whitman's *Leaves of Grass* in 1856, called it an "intensely vulgar, nay, absolutely beastly book"; *Saturday Review* called it "exceedingly obscene" and recommended readers throw it "instantly behind the fire"; and Rufus W. Griswold, writing in *Criterion,* remarked that "it is impossible to imagine how any man's fancy could have conceived such a mass of stupid filth, unless he were possessed of the soul of a sentimental donkey that had died of disappointed love." Reviewers have mocked books ruthlessly, and sometimes hilariously: critiquing the work of Frederic Prokosch, Randall

Jarrell, renowned for his acerbity, said that his poems "pour out like sausages, automatic, voluptuous, and essentially indistinguishable." Even in our own milder era, the *New York Times Book Review* critic lit into Nicholson Baker's novel *Checkpoint* with a blunt appraisal—"This scummy little book"—and in a review of *The Know-It-All: One Man's Humble Quest to Become the Smartest Person in the World,* the *Times* reviewer suggested, none too gently, that the author was a "jackass," while Dale Peck, who has built a reputation on slashing reviews ("hatchet jobs," as he calls them), said of Jim Crace's books that "their lowest-common-denominator dilettantism is the embodiment of everything I despise about contemporary fiction." Cruel reviews can hurt writers, and, if they stop good writers from writing, they can harm literature. But while nastiness has been shunned as unethical by many editors and reviewers, it has not been judged defamatory—unless it is directed at the author rather than the book.[5]

Once reviewers wander into personal terrain, they enter an area where they may be held legally accountable for their opinions. Precedent for this was set as far back as the mid-nineteenth century by a series of libel suits brought against the press by James Fenimore Cooper. These suits, seldom discussed today—and last described in detail, so far as I know, by Ethel R. Outland in *The "Effingham" Libels on Cooper,* published in 1929—took place between 1837 and 1845. Fascinating for the light they shed on Cooper, whom most of us probably associate only with the Leatherstocking Tales, this extended and convoluted litigation took in a variety of issues, including the limits of what can fairly be said in a review.

The reviewing quarrels, as described by Outland, arose from several extraliterary factors.[6] One of these was the affair known as the Three Mile Point controversy, which arose when Cooper decided to close off a local area—Three Mile Point—that had been used by townspeople for recreation but was in fact on his private property. He was harshly criticized for the action by several newspapers and was in the process of suing them for libel when he proceeded to fictionalize the episode in his novel *Home as Found.* Reviewers of this book, rather than simply focusing on the novel, brought in the issue of the controversy, involving their reviews in subsequent libel suits. A second ingredient in the quarrels was Cooper's critical attitude toward Americans, which seems to have developed during the years he lived in Europe and which he expressed in his nonfiction, as well as in the novels *Home as Found* and *Homeward Bound,* alienating both the press and the public that had previously so admired him.

The reviews in question were so hostile that they make Moldea's *Times* review by comparison seem extremely tame. Outland reprints part of one review, which was published in the *New-Yorker* in 1838 and contained what became notorious as the "superlative dolt" passage:

> Mr. Cooper's Last Novel.—After many vigorous struggles to read "Home As Found" with anything like the particularity which is necessary for a criticism, we gave up the attempt in downright despair. It is duller even than "Homeward Bound"; . . . As we promised, however, to give in addition to our remarks, some of those with which Col. Webb of the Courier and Enquirer scorched the testy novelist so unmercifully, we proceed, with what grace we may, to the performance of a disagreeable task.
>
> We differ from Mr. Webb in the opinion that Mr. Cooper's object in villifying his own country and lauding Europe was to make his works saleable in London. Mr. Cooper is too fond of pouring out his bile and venting his spleen, to wait for a motive to induce his course of conduct or writing. When in England, he blackguarded the English; now that he is at home, he blackguards his own countrymen. He is as proud of blackguarding as a fishwoman is of Billingsgate. It is as natural to him as snarling to a tom-cat or growling to a bull-dog.
>
> Finding that people would not buy his books of "Gleanings"— which he put forth as outlets for his pent-up indignation—he resorted to his old trick of novel-making, and took advantage of those forms of literature, under which he had become popular with the American public, to asperse, villify, and abuse that public. But he has not sown the wind without reaping the whirlwind. He is the common mark of scorn and contempt of every well-informed American. The superlative dolt! Did he imagine that he was the only person in the country that had ever traveled in Europe, so that the gross exaggeration of his sketches would not be detected? Did he suppose that no intelligent Englishman had ever moved in our circle of good society, so that his lying caricatures would not be trampled under foot? *Quem Deus vult perdere, prius dementat.* If this adage be true, and Mr. Cooper be not near his ruin, he is the craziest loon that was ever suffered to roam at large without whip and keeper. We respectfully hint to his

friends the necessity of an early application to the benevolent Direc-
tor of the Insane Hospital.

Mr. Webb charges Mr. Cooper with making himself the hero of his
tale under the name of Mr. Effingham; and the charge is irrefragably
maintained.[7]

As Outland observes, "Such were the pleasantries of book reviewing in
1838."[8] (Apparently not a Golden Age of Book Reviewing.)

Vicious as the reviews were, the issue for Cooper was not the negativi-
ty of the criticism. Like Moldea, he was fighting for a principle: Cooper
argued that criticism must be kept within literary bounds. Among the ar-
duous and acrimonious trials that ensued, one included reading aloud
and commenting on both novels—a twenty-one-hour ordeal. Cooper
wisely absented himself from the reading: one newspaper reported that
"five jurymen are supposed to have been carried out fainting." Cooper
won the civil suits that established the "fair comment" principle that he
was fighting for, which affirmed that "the privilege of criticism cannot
warrantably be perverted to the purpose of willfully and falsely assailing
the moral character of the author."[9]

By contrast, Moldea, in his suit, didn't claim that his character had been
assailed, only his book, raising the question of whether a negative review,
if it misrepresented a book, could be considered defamatory. Moldea almost won, when two of the three judges in the U.S. Court of Appeals for
the District of Columbia argued that reviews should be held to the same
standards as a hard news story. But the case was finally decided against him
when the court reversed its earlier decision.

The response of the reviewing community to the Moldea case was
mixed. The National Book Critics Circle, the only organization of reviewers and review editors that might be said to reflect, if not represent, the
views of that community, declined, through its board, to take a stand. On
the one hand, a victory for Moldea might have been disastrous for reviewing. If reviews were held to a hard news standard, critics might be ha-
rassed, fined—jailed!—and court time squandered on points that could
never be decided on the basis of "provable facts." If a reviewer said, "The
dialogue in this novel doesn't ring true," for example, could an author,
claiming that his future as a screenwriter had been ruined, sue, bringing

to court someone who swore that he had in real life spoken exactly those lines, proof that they did "ring true"? Moreover, if publications were held liable for negative opinions, they might well be too nervous to run negative reviews even if critics had the nerve to write them; American criticism, already lacking backbone, would turn to jelly.

On the other hand, Moldea wasn't wrong: the *Times* review was, as Edwin Diamond said, itself a case of "sloppy journalism,"[10] and a decision that reviewers have the legal right to be sloppy didn't seem all that much to cheer about.

It's unfortunate, I think, that Moldea felt compelled to take his case to court, an unsuitable arena for resolving the ambiguities of fairness in reviewing. But he did the field a service by so conspicuously linking fairness and accuracy, a connection that, in reviewing, tends to be overlooked. Most discussions about fairness focus on negative reviewing. Indeed the very term *unfair* seems reserved for negative reviews, especially those that seem overly critical, nasty, or mocking of an author. But this perspective is both narrow and decidedly authorcentric. Obviously, most dustups will erupt when reviews have been critical: Moldea wouldn't have sued the *Times* over a rave review of his book, whatever errors it might have contained, any more than Cooper would have sued the newspapers had their too-personal critiques said his excellent novels proved him to be an upstanding American of high moral character. But there are many ways to be unfair, and inaccuracy, not nastiness, is at the heart of most of them.

The review that overpraises a book isn't judged to be "unfair," though it is of course—to readers, who go out to buy an "extraordinary" work and come home with substandard fare. The review that distorts a book, even if it praises it, is unfair to author, book, and readers alike. And even nastiness often comes down to imprecision. In the fuss stirred up in the literary world by Dale Peck's *New Republic* review of *The Black Veil*, a memoir by Rick Moody, critics pointed repeatedly to Peck's opening line: "Rick Moody is the worst writer of his generation." But they might have paid more attention to another sentence in Peck's "hatchet job": "Stop reading here," Peck told his audience, "if you are looking for a calm dissection of the work of Hiram Frederick Moody III." Reprinting the essay in his book *Hatchet Jobs*, Peck revised this line to read, "an objective or, for that matter, rational dissection of the work,"[11] perhaps to clarify the subjective nature of his criticism. But surely a calm, well-reasoned dissection of the work is exactly what a fair review would be, however subjective. Unless reviewers describe as precisely as possible both the book and their assessment of it, they're bound to misrepresent books and mislead readers. Yet inaccuracy in reviewing is ubiquitous.

At the most basic level, reviews are filled with factual errors. Publishers, dates, page numbers, names of characters, even titles and authors are reported incorrectly with surprising frequency. (In one review of an anthology I edited, I somehow morphed into "Grace Pool"—a case of a reviewer too engrossed in *Jane Eyre,* I assume.)

Obviously, many errors at this level are minor and, however irritating, have no impact on what is being said. Nor is it fair to dismiss an entire review for its trivial mistakes, which aren't necessarily an indication of a reviewer's slovenly reading habits or even perhaps his fault. Although reviewers should be more careful than they are in using press releases, which are routinely inaccurate, and galleys, which are uncorrected proofs printed before the book has been finalized, reviewers aren't responsible for many of the errors that creep in as copy gets processed by editorial and production staff. In a *Houston Post* review I wrote of Paul Bowles's *The Sheltering Sky,* the novel was referred to throughout as "The Skeltering Sky," a mistake that certainly wasn't mine, though I was the one who looked like a fool. But, as my *Post* editor lamented, that such easily correctable errors aren't corrected suggests, not only to readers but to reviewers themselves, that no one really cares and helps create an ethic in which errors are acceptable.

And not all factual errors are so minor. It may not matter enormously if a reviewer misidentifies a publisher. But it probably matters if, in reviewing Milorad Pavić's novel *Dictionary of the Khazars,* the reviewer doesn't realize, as some critics did not, that the Khazars were not the author's invention. It certainly matters if, in reviewing a novel, a critic mistakes a diabetic for a narcotics addict, as Jack Green reported in *Fire the Bastards!* his indictment of the reviewing media. It matters if a reviewer of Frances Sherwood's historical novel about Mary Wollstonecraft, *Vindication,* believes that "What's most remarkable about this fictional biography is that it manages to touch upon so many trendy topics—child abuse, mental illness, homosexuality, and drug addiction—without departing from the basic facts," when Sherwood, by her own admission, did depart from those facts in regard to these trendy topics—making more than one reviewer (myself included) extremely uneasy—and whatever might be remarkable about the novel, it is not its authenticity in these areas. And it most definitely matters if the reviewer of Susan McDougal's *The Woman Who Wouldn't Talk,* a memoir about the controversial Whitewater probe, misreports the outcome of the case that is the subject of the book, as the *New York Times Book Review* critic did, revealing that she knows neither the facts nor the book she's reviewing. In these cases, reviewers, whether they misread, read without adequate background knowledge, or fail to read, end up basing their judgments and interpretations on misperceptions.[12]

But reviewing is never simply a question of "just the facts, ma'am." A review may be informationally correct but wrongheaded all the same. The reviewer who wrote, "It seems that for years John Updike has been undervalued as both a master craftsman and ingenious storyteller"[13]—apparently an inhabitant of an alternate universe—is framing his review in a literary world that doesn't exist. The reviewer who approaches an Ed McBain mystery from the perspective of the literary novel and finds—surprise!—that it lacks the depth of a work by Tolstoy is complaining that his fish doesn't taste like beef. A reviewer needs to find a frame that fits the book, not force the book into an unsuitable frame. What he chooses of course depends upon the book, and more than one approach can work. He might discuss the book in relation to an author's previous work, to comparable works, or to its genre. James Wood, writing in the *New Republic,* astutely discussed the work of Zadie Smith within the context of the contemporary novel. Daniel Mendelsohn, in the *New York Review of Books,* examined Dale Peck's *Hatchet Jobs* within the context of criticism. Michael Dirda, writing in the *Washington Post Book World* about two books by Harry Mathews, discussed them thoughtfully in terms of "difficult" fiction.[14] Each of these critics found a context relevant to broader literary issues as well as to the books under review.

Yet often reviewers impose a context into which the book doesn't really fit, or they muddy the context with comparisons that are inapt, or they lump the book into a category rather than assessing it on its own terms. "Just as certain mystery writers mature into artists—John D. MacDonald and Elmore Leonard come to mind—there are writers of what I will call 'women's fiction' whose real gifts don't flower until midcareer," began a review in the *New York Times Book Review*. "Anne Tyler's early books were charming but slight; the new ones sure aren't slight, and she's earned herself a major place in, if not American literature, then at least American publishing."[15] By this point in the review, readers might well have felt confused, as I did, since, as it happened, the book under review was a novel by Maeve Binchy. The entire opening read as if it might have been crafted primarily to aim its barb at Anne Tyler and introduce the vague genre of "women's fiction," rather than to establish a candid and legitimate approach to the novel that was being discussed.

Although it's seldom viewed as inaccuracy, or as unfairness, reviewers' lavish and reckless use of comparisons between books or authors is both. Every book is distinct, for better or worse, and it's the reviewer's job to convey its distinctness to those who haven't read it. Sometimes a contrast can help do this. When a reviewer at the *Los Angeles Times*, writing about Richard Russo's story collection *The Whore's Child*, says: "Neither a satirist—like Sinclair Lewis—nor an idealizer—like Thornton Wilder—[Russo] plumbs the depths and shallows of small-town existence . . . ,"[16] she is drawing on readers' familiarity with two well-known American writers to help show how Russo deals differently with similar subject matter.

But finding similarity between one author or book and another is rarely the best way to show what makes a work unique, especially when the so-called similarity is farfetched, as it so often is. Scanning an assortment of reviews of Deborah Eisenberg's *Twilight of the Superheroes*, I found that various reviewers compared the author to Eudora Welty, John Cheever, James Salter, Richard Ford, Lorrie Moore, William Trevor, Ingmar Bergman, John Cassavetes, Chekhov (of course), and (twice) Alice Munro. Are any of these comparisons accurate? Are they useful? When in the *Atlantic Monthly*, the reviewer of Alice McDermott's *Child of My Heart*, says of the author: "Her talent is not a messy, capacious one: she is more Jane Austen than George Eliot in her vantage, her temperature, and her concerns,"[17] she sets up a creaky duality that is at once aggrandizing and diminishing, suggesting as it does that to be a woman writer is inevitably to be like Austen or Eliot—not like a male writer, apparently, and not simply one's own writerly self.

Although it's also seldom viewed as inaccuracy, or as unfairness, the sloppy language that permeates reviews fails to represent in any useful way either a book or the reviewer's response to it. It's difficult to describe a book. Indeed, the description has always seemed to me the most challenging part of a review to write, particularly if the work is fiction or poetry. It seems to me still harder in reviewing other arts, such as dance, art, or music, where a critic has to render nonverbal attributes in verbal terms. But if, as Jacques Barzun once said, it's crucial that critics in all the arts use words with "technical precision," that "it is as great a blunder to write *metaphor* for *symbol* or *tension* for *conflict* as it would be for a physicist to use *photon* for *proton*,"[18] book reviewers blunder with abandon. What does it mean to say that a novel "unfolds like an urban legend?"[19] What is "lucid heartbreak"?[20] What is "deadpan pathos"?[21]

Strictly speaking, to say that a book "has changed literature's future" or has "permanently extended the range of the English language" can have no basis in reality. The reviewer, writing in the present, cannot know either of these things. When a reviewer who has said that a book "occasionally becomes tiresome and threatens to sink into a sea of details and acronyms" then proceeds to call the book "compelling,"[22] it becomes clear that the ubiquitous "compelling" is a content-free filler, so clichéd that it's invisible both to the reviewer who used it and to the editor who let it stand. Using off-the-rack adjectives—"impressive" and "astonishing" (first novels), "towering" (achievements), "luminous" (prose)—reviewers slight the books and authors they haven't bothered to characterize and the readers they haven't bothered to edify. Nearly all reviewers are guilty at some time of reviewese—which in "Tom Payne's guide to the words that reviewers and publishers love too much" extends from "achingly beautiful" to "writes like a dream"[23]—and I confess I've contributed my share. But the carelessness makes it seem that reviewers aren't aware of what they're saying, haven't worked out what they want to say, or perhaps don't mean what they do say.

Some level of imprecision is inevitable in reviewing, dealing as it does not only with words, but with words about words, and subject as it is to journalistic pressures. But do reviewers actually have to say things that they don't know? Do they have to say things they know to be untrue? Do they have to use jargon and clichés, drop irrelevant names, and pad with meaningless phrases and sentences? Do editors have to publish everything and anything that reviewers write? Whatever the inevitable level of imprecision, it's clearly raised by the habits and traditions of the field.

It's true that time will never be on the reviewer's side. Editors want currency, and schedules, I've found, are seldom flexible. The actual time reviewers are given to deal with a book will vary with the publication, the editor, the circumstances. They may have a month. Or they may be asked, if they're regular contributors to a publication, to come through quickly with a review of a book which for some reason—another reviewer's illness, difficulty obtaining galleys, an editor's absent-mindedness—fell out of schedule. As a columnist, if a newly arrived book fit well in my forthcoming roundup, under editorial pressure or by choice I might review it within a few days. But the issue isn't whether reviewers have a week or a month, but whether what they have is enough. A month certainly sounds ample, if we imagine someone just reading a book and writing her review. But since a reviewer can't live on a single reviewing fee, most likely (let's hope) he has other work—a job, other kinds of writing, or other reviews which he's working on simultaneously. Reviewers may also have limits on the hours they're willing to put in for their meager fee. And if a review is to be accurate, more is generally required than simply reading the book.

If, without background reading, the nonexpert reviewer may have trouble finding an appropriate context in which to discuss a book, unless he can do some research—at a minimum, some spot-checking to make sure the author is generally reliable—he won't know whether the book he's reviewing is itself accurate. Many are not. "In any nonfiction book . . . it is presumed by the reader that the facts have been checked and are accurate, and that the book therefore is to be relied on," writes Clarkson N. Potter, in *Who Does What and Why in Book Publishing*. "In most publishing houses, however, a copy editor simply cannot check everything. Let us say he is editing a civil war history. For him to check every name, every date, every location, in fact, all the assertions made in the text, would be to do the work of author—presumably an authority—all over again, only without his background."[24] If a copy editor, upon checking, finds an author is generally unreliable, he and the editor will have to "decide how important the book is, how important the author is, and how serious the problem is," says Potter. "A lot of very famous authors are really quite sloppy, and both editor and copy editor simply have to live with it and keep as many obvious errors as possible from slipping through to final copy."[25]

Unfortunately, the reviewer who can't discern the errors, which aren't always readily apparent, also has to live with them. But if the reader presumes that the facts in a book "have been checked and are accurate," the reviewer surely should be more skeptical. His job is to appraise the book, including the quality of its information. In many cases, the nonexpert reviewer, if he were honest, would declare himself unable to do this and comment only on the aspects of the book he could capably judge. But this isn't "done" in American book reviewing, and to do it would discredit the review. Tradition demands that the reviewer *sound* authoritative; apparently, all of us—reviewers, editors, readers—would prefer the myth of reviewer expertise to the truthful admission of limited knowledge.

Still, you would expect that even if a reviewer wasn't able to appraise a book's accuracy, he would want to maintain that of his review and would be careful to attribute to its source information he's passing on: it isn't incorrect to say that Ms. Author says such and such, even if such and such is untrue, nor is it hedging. From an ethical viewpoint, such attribution gives credit where it's due, making it clear that this is the author's research, not the reviewer's; from a critical viewpoint, it establishes the distance reviewers need to maintain between what they're reading and their own commentary, and, most important, allows readers to distinguish between the two. Many reviewers do this scrupulously. But many do not. Whether because they forget to be skeptical, or because it seems clumsy to say repeatedly, "As Jane Author says"—and it can be clumsy unless reviewers write skillfully—or because even this sounds insufficiently authoritative, it has become standard practice for reviewers to simply appropriate the authors' narratives for their own reviews. An author says, dramatically, that "John X was seriously depressed in 1975," and reviewers begin their review, "In 1975, John X was seriously depressed."

In fiction, obviously, this poses no problem; if the reviewer has been accurate, the story he's describing is intrinsically—fictionally, at least—true: if the novelist says that John X was depressed, then, barring an "unreliable narrator," he was. But in nonfiction, the situation is different: the biographer's saying that John X was depressed doesn't automatically make it true, and the reviewer should make it clear that this is the author's version of events. Often, reviewers not only fail to do this but compound the problem by declaring a book "meticulously researched," when in fact they don't know that the research was meticulous, only perhaps that it was voluminous. Unless a reviewer has checked out the book's references and sources, for all he knows—or doesn't know—they could have been fabricated, plagiarized, or misused.

Even for knowledgeable reviewers, the pressure to work quickly can easily lead to errors. Working to deadline, I was always aware that I might read too quickly, take notes too quickly, misread notes, overlook important aspects of a book, miss the subtleties of prose or the niceties of an argument, and make mistakes. I was also aware that there would be no one to catch mistakes, that my editors hadn't read the books I was reviewing, that no editors could so carefully read all the books reviewed on their book pages. As Jack Miles, the former editor of the *Los Angeles Times Book Review,* observed in an article about the Moldea case:

> The body of information for which the editor of the *New York Times Book Review* is somehow responsible during any given period exceeds in its size and complexity the body of information for which the editor of the *New York Times* as a whole is otherwise responsible during the same period. If the standards of accuracy that the newspaper maintains for its reporters should be required for its reviewers, a fact-checking staff large enough to, in effect, re-review each book in-house would be required.[26]

But, judging by our reviews, editors seldom take advantage of even their limited opportunities to catch errors. They let stand the careless writing that, as every editor knows, is usually a sign of careless reading and thinking. They don't demand that a reviewer attribute his information and clearly distinguish between what he is saying and what Ms. Author said, which in itself would encourage all reviewers to pay close attention to what Ms. Author did say. And few editors in my experience request second advance copies of the books they know they'll be reviewing, which would enable them at least to check reviewers' quotes. While it's true that even this can be only moderately helpful—editors won't be able to grasp enough of the context to judge how the quote has been applied—it would at least enable them to gauge whether a reviewer is obviously careless, someone to watch in the future or perhaps to avoid. And like everyone else, reviewers who know that something will be checked are more likely to be careful.

In one sense, of course, within the framework of reviewing, no amount of time would be enough. For reviewers, however careful, the short interval between reading and comment dooms them to imprecision: this is the nature of reviewing, reviewers can see books only close-up. Not only do they lack the historical perspective available to the critic dealing with older books, they lack even the weeks that they know are likely to alter their own first impressions. With fiction in particular the immediate response often proves unreliable. Rereading my past reviews, I'm amazed at how many quiet books have stayed with me, while books that seemed powerful when I read them apparently had more style than substance and have faded from memory. In nonfiction as well, over time, holes appear in what seemed to be tightly knit arguments; the verbal strings that were pulled unravel.

All reviewers sometimes have second thoughts, but by then their opinions have been published. In an article called "Second Thoughts," David Ansen, *Newsweek*'s movie critic, revised downward his original opinion of Steven Spielberg's *Minority Report* because, he said, "where some movies grow stronger and richer in retrospect, 'Minority Report' has distinctly diminished in my mind." In reviewing movies, and even more in reviewing live performances, critics need to make assessments far more quickly than do book reviewers, who can at least reread the text. The theater critic Harold Clurman once observed that he adjusted the tenor of his opinions allowing for the time interval. "My notices in the weeklies tended to be milder than those I wrote for the monthly," he said, "and I suspect that I should be more careful to be kind if I wrote for a daily." His work in theater, he observed, had taught him "many lessons about snap judgments and the dangers of a too proud or rigid dogmatism."[27]

That reviewers have forgotten this most basic premise of reviewing is evident when they call books "instant classics" and predict their impact on "the future of literature" or its ultimate decline. And editors, apparently forgetful as well, don't ask them to put away their crystal balls. I'm not suggesting that reviewers, aware that their vision is limited, shouldn't express strong opinions or that passion isn't welcome. But hype isn't passion, and vitriol isn't criticism: a book needn't be a candidate for vaporization if it seems to fail, and it doesn't have to "change literature" to be good, an old-fashioned word that I would love to see revived.

Nowhere is the time frame of reviewing more problematic than when reviewers deal with innovative works and try to sort out the authentic from the vaporware, to interpret the new. This is surely one of the art critic's most important roles, and Jack Green was right to be outraged by the reviews of Gaddis's *The Recognitions,* not because reviewers didn't like it but because in dismissing this long, difficult work without having read it very well—or, in some cases, at all—they failed to take on the role of interpreter. But it's demanding to deal with books that, as one early reviewer observed of Whitman's *Leaves of Grass,* set "all the ordinary rules of criticism at defiance," and "must be read again and again."[28] Reviewers need time to read books "again and again," they need space for complex observations, they need the taste and temperament for experimental work or they'll be all too likely to grow angry at the book for being difficult, as some of Gaddis's reviewers seem to have done, or feel so at sea that they'll simply choose to say something favorable, which may have little to do with what they think but will at least, it may seem, do no harm.

Too often, though, if a book is being touted as a "literary event," the "new *Ulysses,*" editors, under pressure to be current, find it hard to allow extra time. If the book is obscure, and unlikely to appeal to a large audience, editors sometimes feel—if they assign it at all—that it doesn't warrant extra space. The *New York Times Book Review* allowed so little room for its brief review of Harry Mathews's *The Human Country* that the reviewer could say nothing about Mathews's background as the only American member of the French workshop Oulipo (Ouvroir de Littérature Potentielle) and gave no real sense of the experimental aspect of his fiction. And while I'm sure that many editors do try to match innovative books with suitable reviewers, editors have certainly sent me such works without inquiring about my taste or interest—indeed, without even mentioning the books' experimental nature. And again, our reviewing ethic doesn't support reviewers admitting to their own uncertainty out of fear that to do so might undermine their critical authority. It's the rare and confident reviewer who seems able to admit not only to the difficulty of a book, but even to his own incomplete comprehension, as Michael Dirda did in his review of Harry Mathews's work. I admit I've never been able to do it myself. But Dirda's approach enabled him to be critical without sounding dismissive, to be appreciative without sounding dishonest, and to prepare readers for the difficulty they themselves would encounter.[29]

Space is an issue for all reviews, not only those that deal with difficult literature, and while space alone solves nothing if it isn't well used, a lack of it can intensify the problems created by lack of time. Few reviewers have the room allowed in the *New York Review of Books* or the *New Republic,* which offer critics several thousand words for a review. At newspapers, I usually had five hundred to one thousand words and for a column, those one thousand words were expected to cover several books. As a reader, I happen to like shorter reviews—when they're good. But as a reviewer, I know how hard they are to pull off. Writing short is harder than writing long. The underlying work has always seemed to me the same: reviewers have to work out the careful argument whether or not they have room to present it, or they'll find themselves saying things they couldn't defend if they had to. And if, without time, even reviewers who know their response to a book may have trouble analyzing the reasons for it, without space, even if they've identified the reasons, they may have trouble compressing all they have to say. A brief review can't ramble toward its conclusions: in a five-hundred-word critique I knew I had to make even the punctuation count. And without room for clauses, a review is inevitably dependent on adjectives, which, as any writing teacher will tell you, are weak.

But too often what gets squeezed out in the compression are the particulars of description and assessment, the very heart of the review. Short of space, reviewers turn to shortcuts, such as the comparisons they hope will quickly identify the books they're discussing, managing only to waste some of what little space they have. Dependent on adjectives, and lacking time to find the right ones, they reach for the familiar clichés—"compelling," "astonishing," "stunning," "flawed"—which are nonspecific and can be applied, or misapplied, with impunity to any book, since they essentially serve as code words for the reviewer's general response: I liked this; that, I didn't. And because in the authorcentric world of American reviewing, we tend to feel that praise can stand on its own, but criticism needs to be explained, if a complex criticism can't be defended in the five hundred words, a reviewer will often omit it altogether, if she likes the book at all, though this leaves a false impression of her fuller assessment.

Editors, I've found, don't discourage these things. In my experience, most editors are more comfortable with praise than with criticism and have accepted my judgment that a book was "wonderful" on the basis of minimal evidence but were more concerned that my criticisms be justified. And whatever editors may think of the use of clichés and irrelevant author comparisons, that they publish them with such frequency suggests widespread tolerance. Editors themselves of course lack time, they may be faced with editorial problems more serious than a bit of jargon, and realistically they need publishable reviews, not perfect ones—as an editor once told me outright, she preferred the right date to the right word. But I've had editors actually suggest, when I was stuck for an adjective, that I use "compelling" and recommend that I come up with the name of some book "like" the one I was reviewing, saying that information might be "helpful" to readers. It's my impression that editors take the view that clichés, jargon, and other forms of reviewese are mediocre prose rather than inaccuracy and that reviewers who use them are writing badly rather than saying things that aren't true.

Finally, beyond the constraints of deadlines and word counts, a reviewer needs to create a piece of writing that is interesting in its own right and yet true to the book, a double task that can be daunting. For one thing, in American reviewing, "interesting" is often construed to mean "lively," the kind of writing that's so snappy it can draw even readers who aren't interested in the book, or even perhaps in books. But books for the most part, even good ones, don't readily lend themselves to attention-grabbing liveliness, and reviewers can create it only artificially, by contriving something catchy or by overheating the importance of a book, its subject, or, most often, its quality, especially in their opening paragraphs and conclusions. This leads to the familiar hype—"exquisite," "gorgeous," "profound," "his best yet," "never before," "never again"—which descriptions and discussions must (often falsely) live up to; and to the contrived angles (such as Updike as undervalued craftsman) which take reviewers and readers boldly in the wrong direction.

Carol Shields was certainly right to praise the reviews of Eudora Welty, for "the simplicity" of their "opening sentences," which Shields observed are "a rebuke to those reviewers who stand on their heads to be clever"; she cited such lines as "This is a book of twenty-one short stories," "These are stories and sketches collected from writings over a period of several years," and "This is a disarming book, and a pleasure to read."[30] Such openings focus attention, as they should, on the books, and they are unlikely to lead readers—or reviewers themselves—astray. But I see few such straightforward leads in our reviews, and I suspect that many editors would consider them flat—I can even recall an editor requesting that I rewrite one such plain opening, which she found in need of some pizzazz.

Clearly if reviews are going to be read, they do need to be interesting. But often, what is most distinctive about the book, which ought to frame the discussion, may be something that the reviewer can't use. It may be that what is most significant in the book will be of little interest to the general reader. In literature, books often succeed or fail for essentially technical reasons that are interesting to those who are interested but pretty dry in journalistic terms. Do fiction readers really want to hear about narrative structure or the use of indirect discourse? Yet for many novels, to talk about story, which makes for lively copy, is critically irrelevant. Sometimes what is significant about a book is an aspect of the work the reviewer isn't equipped to handle, and the problem is the wrong reviewer. Or a book lacks the coherence to permit a coherent description and discussion, and the book shouldn't have been chosen for review. Or there is nothing distinctive about the dull book except the fact that it was chosen, and again, it shouldn't have been, but the work for which the reviewer is responsible—the review—has to be interesting nonetheless. In any of these cases, the discussion ends up skewed.

The likelihood that the discussion will be distorted is still higher when a reviewer has several books to consider together, a popular form of assignment. From the editor's perspective, such groupings are practical: he needs to find only one reviewer, he can pay him less than he would have to pay two or three, and he can efficiently use limited space to cover several books at once in a category judged to be of lesser popularity (poetry) or of lesser importance (mysteries). And a discussion of several related books can create an interesting essay, opening up a broad discussion of a subject: as an editor I always had an eye out for interesting pairs or trios of books, and I understand why editors can't resist combining several books on global warming, presidential politics, or women in the workplace that have been published in a single season.

But having written many double-book reviews and roundup columns, I know all too well the strain of finding a way of talking about them all that does justice to each. Auden noted the distortion that occurs if a reviewer

> has to review four poets in the same article and . . . they are all of them quite good, which means that the work of each is unique. If he treats them as such, then his article has no focus. But an article must have a focus. So he invents one. He looks for some characteristic which they have in common—it may be something as trivial as their

age—and gives this a label—the X School, the Y Generation, the Z Young Men, etc.—and writes his article around it. The Publishers are delighted—it is easier to sell packages—and so is the Public delighted—labels save it from thinking and provide it with party conversation. Everybody, in fact, is pleased except the unfortunate poets.[31]

Even when the books fit well together, what is distinctive about one may not be the way in which it relates to the other(s), but something entirely different. And there is no question that books read differently in close proximity to others. I felt sympathy for the *Women's Review of Books* critic whose joint review of May Sarton's journal and Doris Grumbach's memoir, which initially must have seemed an inspired matchup, drew angry letters from Sarton, who felt that the reviewer "lumps old women together"; from Grumbach, who felt that "portmanteau reviews of this sort hurt both the writer of the book praised (to some extent) and the one treated more harshly"; and from a reader, who felt that such a pairing is "inherently unfair to the authors since it lends itself to a contest mentality: *who wins?*"[32] Certainly, as the critic in this quarrel argued, considering two texts together can enhance the discussion of both. Neither book has to win. But since comparison is, at least in part, the point of the pairing, and even similar books are neither equivalent nor equal, fair treatment of both will be tricky.

But the review is almost sure to go astray when the grouping itself is artificial. I never had to face the situation of Orwell's hapless reviewer who, when he rips open the "bulky parcel containing five volumes which his editor has sent with a note suggesting that they 'ought to go well together,' finds "*Palestine at the Cross Roads, Scientific Dairy Farming, A Short History of European Democracy* (this one is 680 pages and weighs four pounds), *Tribal Customs in Portuguese East Africa,* and a novel, *It's Nicer Lying Down,* probably included by mistake."[33] But I have had to wrestle with various groupings that are often treated as categories, such as first fiction, novels-written-by-women, and poetry-written-by-anyone, which aren't, in fact, meaningful categories and would inevitably include books that could only be yoked together by invention.

Distortions, in reviewing, are bound to occur: reviewers bring their biases, idiosyncrasies, taste, and limitations to books that have biases, idiosyncrasies, taste, and limitations of their own. Errors are inevitable when masses of information are processed quickly with insufficient checks. If journalism is an imperfect craft, reviewing is surely one of its least perfectible divisions. But it's easy, I think, to take shelter in the sanctity of "opinion" and in dismissing liability to dismiss accountability as well. Neither the shield of opinion nor the force of journalistic pressures quite excuses the inaccuracy that seems entirely acceptable in reviewing, though in axing credibility and fairness, it does a hatchet job of its own.

Private Opinions, Public Forums

... in a period when bad books receive more acclaim than ever—and when good books, if they do succeed in being published, are often lost in the shuffle—it can sometimes be a critic's moral obligation to be "nasty." But many literary folk do not see it this way: talking privately to some critics, one is astonished by the disparity between what they say in conversation about a given book or writer and what they say in print.

—Bruce Bawer, "Literary Life in the 1990s," *New Criterion*, September 1991

The curious element in our American situation is this divorce between the judgments of private conversation and the conventional banalities of the published literary column.

—Bliss Perry, "The American Reviewer," *Yale Review*, October 1914

If our public reviewing were to reach the level of our literary gossip, we would be putting a better foot forward than we do, as a national culture, right now.

—John Hollander, "Some Animadversions on Reviewing," *Daedalus*, 1963

Several years ago I agreed to review a first novel which had already received a few highly placed raves and which was written by a critic whose own reviews my assigning editor said she admired. As it turned out I found the book a workmanlike effort, a decently written but uninspired piece of prose. I neither liked nor disliked it intensely, but in the end I gave it a mostly favorable—i.e., dishonest—write-up and felt so guilty I almost vowed never to review again. This certainly wasn't the first time in twenty years that I had failed to say exactly what I thought of a book or had told the truth but told it slant. But I'd been so determined not to repeat the duplicity that I felt defeated, a recidivist who, I feared, would always be susceptible to the pressures that encourage reviewers to make books out to be better than they think they are.

That reviewers say one thing in private and write another has been a long-standing source of cynicism, humor, anger, and scorn. "The next time you bump into a book critic at a party, ask what he or she has read in the past six months that's really blown their hair back, that they've really admired," wrote Dwight Garner in "Crisis in Critville: Why You Can't Trust Book Reviews," which appeared in the online magazine *Salon*. "Chances are they'll be stumped—at least long enough for you to refill your drink—even if they've written a heap of glowing reviews during that time." In print, said Garner, they may have "purred" over one book or another; "in person, they get cagey."[1]

That private opinions change on the way to the forum, that they tend to grow muted as they mutate, seems shocking, even to the reviewers who are culpable. And yet neither is inexplicable to anyone who looks beyond the reviewer at her desk. Reviewing may be a solitary activity, but it isn't a private affair. When I first began reviewing, I imagined myself alone in my study, reading and responding to a book. But as I should have realized, reviewers aren't hired merely to express their personal opinions but to write something designed for public consumption; and as I quickly discovered, I wasn't quite alone in that room. In the shadows were the editor who had hired me, the periodical publisher who had hired him, the publishing house, the author, readers, and, an alternate persona, the Reviewer, with a career and reputation to consider. The context for reviews is commercial, American culture largely anti-intellectual, and American readers egalitarian, wary of criticism, and not deeply in love with books—as the publishing historian Donald Sheehan observed, "Whatever the glories of the American home, a large and well-used library has not been among them."[2]

Freelance reviewers say they're self-employed, but this is essentially a tax category; they're working for the publications which publish their reviews and which have cultural and commercial aims that influence the kinds of reviews they publish. This seems to me self-evident, yet when I remarked once, on a criticism panel, that as editor of a literary magazine, I expected our reviewers to write for our audience, the comment enraged one of my fellow panelists, a popular-music critic for the *Boston Globe*, who objected that critics don't write for an audience. It wasn't clear whether he thought I meant that critics should tailor their opinions to suit our editorial viewpoint, which I did not mean, or to suit our advertisers' needs, which would have been absurd since, like most literary magazines, we had almost no advertisers; but if he thought that one review fits all, he was surely wrong.

It's highly unlikely that this critic's music reviews for the *Boston Globe* would have been published as is in *Rolling Stone* and impossible that my reviews for the *Cleveland Plain Dealer* would have appeared as is in the *New York Review of Books*. Comparing two reviews of Fiona MacCarthy's *Byron: Life and Legend,* which were published in the *Times Literary Supplement* and the daily *New York Times,* I find the contrasts so striking from their opening paragraphs that it's clear that more than a difference in reviewers is involved.

In the *TLS,* the reviewer begins:

> Virginia Woolf claimed that there is no such thing as an objective biography. "Positions have been taken, myths have been made." This is unquestionably the case with biographies of Byron apart from the early *Byron: A portrait* by Leslie Marchand (1971). William St. Clair describes Professor Marchand's methods thus: "the scrupulous effort to transcribe, to understand and conceptualize the original documents, to reconstruct the essential facts and to allow Byron to speak for himself. Seldom has a biographer been more modest, keeping well in the background, avoiding unnecessary and definitive judgements and offering no overarching psychological or theoretical explanations." The most recent biographers of Byron (and many of those who reviewed their controversial biographies for the newspapers) were more concerned with their own overarching psychological explanations and with shallow judgements (presented as definitive) than with any determined attempt to reconstruct the essential facts from the evidence or to allow Byron to speak for himself and fight his own way out of the layers of myth.[3]

The *New York Times* reviewer begins:

> Lord Byron was the Mick Jagger of his time, "mad, bad, and dangerous to know," in the words of his tragic admirer Caroline Lamb. He was a curly-haired, pouty-lipped heartthrob, though inclined to

plumpness and a dieter and exerciser worthy of the twenty-first century, according to this biography by Fiona MacCarthy. Byron was a celebrity entertainer if there ever was one. The first edition of "Childe Harold's Pilgrimage" was a sensation and sold out in three days. Like any modern entertainer controlling his press, Byron carefully tailored his image, urging his publisher to destroy unattractive portraits of him.[4]

Not quite the same. Each of these reviewers is writing for a particular publication with a particular identity and perceived audience. Both address the myths surrounding Byron's life. But the *TLS* reviewer, like the *TLS* itself, aims to be intellectual; assuming that her readers are themselves intellectual and will find "liveliness" in intellectual issues, she grounds her essay in questions of biography. Since she is writing for a demanding publication and audience, she establishes a context and her expertise at once by referring to relevant works in the field. And since she has plenty of room, and is writing for a weekly supplement, she takes time to set up her essay, apparently unafraid that her readers, primarily English, will lose interest or patience.

The *New York Times* reviewer, however, is writing for a daily newspaper and an American audience, who is likely to be reading her review before work and whose time, patience, and intellectual interest she assumes are limited. Since she has less space, she moves directly to the book and tries to lure her readers in with something lively: but what she considers "lively" is not Virginia Woolf or Professor Marchand, but Mick Jagger; not the question of mythification, but the myth itself, the "curly-haired, pouty-lipped heartthrob" who was "mad, bad, and dangerous to know"; not complex, convoluted prose but a vocabulary designed to grab attention— "tragic," "celebrity," "image," "sensation."

It's inevitable and appropriate that reviewers should craft different reviews for different publications, and theoretically the context should have no impact on their actual assessment. In practice though it can. The reviewer who is writing for an intellectually demanding publication might put more demands upon the book itself, might actually read it differently than she would if she were writing for a lighter-weight publication, and might arrive at a different evaluation of the book. As Harold Clurman said, the reviewer writing for a daily, weekly, or monthly publication might—without forfeiting "honesty" or "high standards"—adjust the tenor of his assessment to allow for the variable intervals he has for reflection.[5] The reviewer who is looking at the book from the perspective of a special-interest publication—the *Women's Review of Books* or *National Review*—might see it differently through the zoom lens than she would through a wide-angle lens. And newspapers, magazines, and Web sites, both collectively and individually, exert different pressures on reviewers that may lead them to say that books are better or, less often, worse than they think they are.

Reviewers writing for newspapers are writing for a medium with distinct aims, demands, and traditions. In America, the daily press from early on included literary criticism as one of its functions, first publishing book notices, which took the form of announcements or advertisements, and later, with the expansion of book publishing, a reading public, and book advertising, printing longer reviews. Historically newspapers have been the most widely read review media for all the arts, and there's no question that this has provided a cultural service. Certainly by bringing news about new books to their large audiences, they've been useful to both readers and publishers. But whether reviewing's berth in newspapers has benefited its development is debatable.

To begin with, newspapers are chiefly in the business of delivering news, most particularly hard news, on such topics as government, international relations, and domestic and local affairs. It is on news coverage, the state of the world not the state of the novel, that newspapers make their living and are judged to succeed or fail; that they've published book reviews has remained a minor factor. In John Tebbel's *Compact History of the American Newspaper*, there are no index entries for book reviewing or literary criticism; in Chalmers M. Roberts's *The Washington Post: The First 100 Years*, there is only a single index entry related to reviewing, one reference to the *Post*'s *Book World*.[6]

One consequence of the primacy of news is that within the newspaper hierarchy the book page is destined to enjoy—or not to enjoy very much—lesser status. In practice, this means not only less prestige but also less support. If most papers do not provide the book page editor with a staff, some do not even grant the books editor a full-time position: an editor may have to double up in another role—perhaps as the movie re-

viewer, or, as was the case at the *San Diego Union-Tribune* when I wrote
for them, as the fashion editor. This double duty cuts into the time editors
have to do their jobs, to choose books carefully, to work with reviewers, or
to edit reviews, let alone to check them for accuracy.

In an underfunded and underappreciated department, review editors
lack clout. They haven't the power to raise reviewer fees, however much
they might like to do so. Reviews are assigned little space, or they're given
inappropriate space: a review may run with the obituaries, for example,
where no one is likely to look for it or notice it and where it seems to serve
as filler. Unlike news, which is essential, book reviews are under pressure
to earn their keep: publishers have sought advertising support, which has
commercialized the book page. Confronting hard times in recent years,
newspapers cut book pages, which not only lack the primacy of news, but
also enjoy neither the popularity of sports sections nor the ad revenues of
entertainment sections. These pressures can lead review editors to seek favorable reviews that will justify the use of space to their own editors, news-
papermen who aren't necessarily bookish types and may believe that selecting a book only to find fault with it is to waste valuable column inches.

Equally important, newspapers' focus on news has led American papers
in various ways to treat books as news, striving for such qualities as ob-
jectivity, newsworthiness, and timeliness, which are news values not intrinsically linked to literary criticism and are not always appropriate, ben-
eficial, or even possible in a literary context.

When Alfred S. Ochs launched the *New York Times Book Review* in 1896,
he made it clear in his instructions to his literary editor that he hoped to
bring to literary news the impartiality the paper strove for in hard news.
But the impartiality required for valid newsgathering and reporting has
mixed value when applied to the book page. Readers have benefited from
newspapers' efforts to be evenhanded in their selection of books and reviewers, from their general policy of nonpartisanship in political or aesthetic matters. But treating "books" as if it were a beat to be covered by reporters whose job is mainly to announce the book's arrival and give an
account of its contents—to provide an objective report—is neither feasi-
ble nor desirable. As the critic John Gross, writing in the *New York Times
Book Review* on its one hundredth anniversary, observed: "Reviewing can
never be reduced to a matter of neutral reporting, since a major part of
the 'news' about any book is how good it is. Even a summary of its contents, except at the most rudimentary level, is likely to involve judgments

and preferences."[7] Not only is "complete impartiality," as Gross suggests, "a mirage," but the effort to achieve it leads reviewers to turn out bland book reports rather than acute critiques—a problem with which readers of the *Times* and the many papers that have emulated it have always struggled.

Newsworthiness, a crucial factor in determining what should or should not be covered in the news, is an uneven yardstick in selecting books for review. In books, newsworthy and noteworthy aren't synonymous. A new book on Goya may be extraordinary, but in newspaper terms it's unlikely to be considered newsworthy enough for a review. A new book about the president, a work on a topical subject, a novel written by a celebrity or celebrated author, any book that has generated "buzz"—these are newsworthy titles, no matter how mediocre the books themselves may actually be, and they have tended to receive the most coverage, leaving little room for the noteworthy. As a focus, the newsworthy angle may be so irrelevant to the book as a book that it distorts the review: the first novel reviewed because it earned a record-breaking advance is likely to be reviewed in light of that advance, a nonliterary factor against which the book is inappropriately measured.

The timeliness central to the concept and quality of newspapers exerts an exaggerated pressure on reviews, which lack a comparable urgency. "Yesterday's news wraps today's fish," runs the adage, but literature, as Pound said, is "news that stays news." Timeliness does matter in reviews: the publisher wants to create interest when a book hits the bookstores; the editor hopes the new book will draw readers to the book page; and the bookstore owner gives such short shelf life to a book that a review several months late might arrive after the book has already vanished from the shelves. But these are publishing issues—matters of commerce not content. I've always felt that there's something out of proportion in the need newspapers have felt to review books as soon as they're out, as if a few additional weeks would be detrimental, and that there's something faintly silly about beating a pub date and "scooping" other book pages, as newspapers have sometimes done, as if to publish the first review of a book mattered. And the deadline mentality can discourage reviewers from the necessary reflection, emphasizing speed over thoughtfulness and careful writing and bringing to the fore the ephemerality of the medium and of their own work.

Finally, newspapers address a mass audience, and though reviewers are probably writing for only a small, well-educated segment of the newspaper's readership, they're expected like other reporters to write as though they were addressing every reader. On this basis, reviewers can't assume any literary knowledge: if they mention Theodore Dreiser, they're supposed to identify him at once as "the author of *An American Tragedy*," if they mention E. M. Forster, they should immediately mention *Howards End* ("soon to be a major motion picture"), and they probably shouldn't mention Harry Mathews at all. They can't assume a grasp of sophisticated or even complex language: At the *Cleveland Plain Dealer,* my editor advised me to keep my sentences and paragraphs short, warning that if I didn't, copyeditors might shorten them for me, and I might not find their cropping an enhancement to style or meaning. Because they're expected to address all readers, reviewers can't even assume interest, which is part of the reason for those catchy leads, a necessity in any case since newspapers are breakfast reading and, as the *New York Times* critic Christopher Lehmann-Haupt once noted, "you have to grab the attention of a reader who is probably being distracted by the fact that his toast is burned."[8] Writing within this constricted, simplified framework, the reviewer may find it hard to say what he wants and may find himself saying something entirely different instead.

To some degree, of course, book page conditions will vary among newspapers, depending on such factors as the size of the publication, its economic health, the abilities and power of the editor who presides over it. But these variations don't alter the fundamental conditions that are traditionally, in some cases inherently, aspects of American newspapers. Newspapers in this country make up an extremely coherent medium, within which reviewers write, producing a recognizable entity: a newspaper review. Reviews written for one newspaper can easily appear in any other, and they regularly do through syndicated news or review services. Similar in their bland style and their tendency toward favorable assessment, these reviews have been molded by similar expectations and restrictions, which editors needn't even articulate: reviewers write the reviews they're accustomed to reading.

Reviewers writing for magazines will also feel the influence of the medium, though it's harder to generalize about a field that encompasses *Vogue,* the *Nation,* and *Scientific American,* all of which carry book reviews. Mag-

azines which, like newspapers, published criticism early on, have generally provided a superior environment for reviewing. Published on weekly,
biweekly, monthly, or bimonthly schedules, magazines have never faced
the constraints imposed by daily editions, and most have been free of the
breaking-news atmosphere that permeates the newsroom. Review editors
can give more time to the entire review process: selecting books, matching them with reviewers, editing reviews. Reviewers generally are given
more time for their assignments. Edited for select audiences, magazines
can offer reviewers sophisticated, interested readers, sparing them the
need to aim for mass appeal and allowing them to write as intelligently or
knowledgeably as they can. Less ephemeral, less shreddable, and better
bound than newspapers, they offer reviewers a more attractive and lasting
medium. Better indexed and, as national rather than local publications,
more widely distributed, they help build critical reputations and offer reviewers a more substantial and prestigious forum.

Not surprisingly, in view of these advantages, magazines historically
have carried much of our best criticism. But the economics of magazine
publishing have limited the ability of most magazines to create and sustain such criticism. While magazines are supported both by circulation
and advertising, they traditionally acquire the major part of their revenues
from advertising and actually underprice the publication in relation to its
cost with a view to building either a large or, in more recent decades, an
especially desirable audience to attract advertisers. Obviously, this approach makes magazines heavily dependent on advertisers, but to break
free of this dependence they would have to raise subscription and single-
copy prices considerably, a risk that might not pay off: people are accustomed to getting magazines relatively inexpensively, and habits like that
are hard to change. And readers have other media they could turn to if
they found magazines too expensive, including the Web, most of which
has been free.

For reviewing, this economic pattern has been unfortunate, since we are
not a bookish culture, and publishers haven't generally supported serious
reviewing with advertising. On the one hand, it has made it hard for reviews in magazines to earn their keep. In magazines for which book reviewing is not the primary focus, reviews, which don't attract substantial
ad revenues or a large proportion of readers, will enjoy lesser status than
other editorial sections. As in newspapers, they're often given inappropri-

ate and inadequate space, relegated with other arts criticism to the "back of the book"—a term that has always reminded me of "back of the bus"— and sometimes kept so short they seem more like notices than reviews. As in newspapers, the need to attract readers to an undernoticed department encourages reviewers to write snappily, to overheat their prose and inflate their praise. The shortage of space exerts pressure to "use it well," i.e., to recommend books, and if you can't find books you like, to like the books you find.

On the other hand, these economic patterns have made it hard for independent book review magazines, the one place where reviewing is intrinsically central, to survive. For all the frustration people have expressed through the years with the quality of the *New York Times Book Review,* no independent general-interest book review magazine has yet drummed up the readers and advertisers to compete with it in coverage, frequency, or availability. The most established of our independent book reviews, the *New York Review of Books,* which was started during a *Times* strike in 1963 as an alternative to the *Times,* found success by identifying an intellectual audience that university press advertisers wanted to reach. But the *New York Review,* with its academic style, nonfiction focus, and liberal slant, is neither general-interest nor politically disinterested. It isn't a forum where reviewers of any stripe discuss books of every kind.

Most of our independent book reviews have been impoverished, struggling with small circulations and little advertising, which limits their income; with bimonthly or quarterly publication, which prohibits timeliness; and with limited distribution, which restricts their visibility and impact. Like other magazines in recent decades, some of our independent book reviews have seen specialization as the path to survival. Such magazines as the *Women's Review of Books, Black Book Review, Black Issues Book Review,* or the *Gay and Lesbian Review* have addressed readers who share a cultural identity, whose books have generally received less attention in the mainstream review media, and who might draw advertisers interested in reaching their particular niche. Whatever the commercial possibilities of this approach (the *Women's Review of Books* in the past few years has struggled to sustain publication), editorially, reviewers who write for these magazines are looking at books through the prism of their specialization. How this plays out will depend upon an individual editor's policies. When I reviewed for the *Women's Review of Books,* writing mostly about fiction, I was never asked to emphasize feminist issues when they weren't pertinent to the book I was reviewing, nor was I expected to praise a book simply because it was written by a woman. Nonetheless I was writing within the context of a feminist magazine, and I certainly gave thought to what would be of interest to my readers.

But whether specialized or general interest, all magazines provide the context in which reviewers write. It isn't chance that reviews in the *New York Review of Books* or the *New Republic* are often provocative; as intellectually prestigious publications, they want provocative commentary, and reviewers will use their space to be provocative—in the best sense, to be intelligent and probing, and in the worst, to be controversial even if their commentary isn't about the book under review. It isn't chance that reviews in the *New Criterion* are often hostile; the magazine is trying to win what it sees as a culture war, and reviewers, who are in any case preaching to the converted, will often use their space to score points rather than to write balanced critiques. Nor is it chance that the *Atlantic Monthly,* which has in recent years paid increasing attention to books, offers a book section that treats books thoughtfully as a part of cultural life. If magazines, unlike newspapers, don't share editorial aims, they do have editorial aims, and book reviews fit within them.

If it's difficult to generalize about magazines as an environment for reviewing, it's still harder to generalize about the Web, which is not only enormously diversified, but also a young medium whose economic and cultural traditions are still taking shape. Compared to print media, the Web is more easily accessible for publishers, more widely available to readers, and less expensive for both. Publications are cheaper to produce, deliver, and promote online, without the cost of printing, postage, or distribution, and book reviews have flourished: on personal Web sites devoted to individuals' opinions about books; on book reviewing Web sites such as Bookreporter.com, which serve as independent reviewing services; on bookselling Web sites, most notably Amazon.com and BarnesandNoble .com, which can afford to devote a vast amount of space to reviews.

But if the Web isn't costly to use, neither is it as yet generally profitable. Indeed, the main shared tradition to date in this diverse medium has been the trouble Web-based enterprises have had finding a way to be lucrative. So far, it has proven difficult to persuade readers to pay for features that were initially offered free and to persuade advertisers to pay to reach audiences whose numbers, interests, and incomes are hard to determine. In this environment, reviewing, intimately familiar with unprofitability, has fit right in. But a field that has suffered in print from inadequate funding hasn't benefited online from having still less. Underpaid in print, reviewers and even editors are often unpaid on the Web; a volunteer corps, they can devote even less time and fewer resources to quality, and they have fewer incentives to do so. Whether because it has been free, because it is new, or because of its egalitarian character as a place where everyone has the right to an opinion and all opinions carry equal weight, the Web has so far lacked the literary status of print: although critics who already have status have reviewed for such online magazines as *Salon* and *Slate*, writing for the Web has yet to become the way for a book reviewer to establish a critical reputation.

Because it's accessible and affordable, the Web does allow for the truly independent reviewer: the individual who sets up a personal Web site for his reviews is, in a literal sense, self-employed and can say precisely what he wants, though whether we can call it "employment" is dubious if he earns no money, and whether he'll be heard is a question. These Web sites, like zines, the self-published magazines which they most closely resemble, have had low visibility; unsupported by the links of more established Web sites, they're harder to find; unendorsed, they're less likely to be trusted and used.

But apart from their own pages, reviewers are writing for particular Web sites and, as with magazines, the editorial aims of an individual site determine the nature of its reviews. Reviewers writing for the more literary online magazines assume and write for a sophisticated audience. Reviewers writing for the many genre sites assume and write for an audience of fans, who may be more enthusiastic than discriminating. Reviewers writing for review sites that are struggling to attract circulation and advertising may find themselves asked to be more upbeat than critical. Web site editors can be extremely forthright in their demands. "Reviews are not editorial or literary critiques," proclaimed the publisher of one online publication in her essay "The Art of Reviewing: Book Reviewing Today"; "published reviews are recommendations for readers to buy the book."[9] Reviewers for this publication, happily now defunct, would respect this mix of egalitarianism and commercialism or, presumably, not be welcome as reviewers.

Even the bookselling sites, the most visible review pages on the Web, influence the reviews that they run, which include—besides reprints from the trade publications (*Publishers Weekly, Kirkus, Booklist*)—two kinds of original critiques: reviews written by their own hired reviewers, and reader commentary.

The first group offers a kind of commentary which, by tradition, wouldn't appear in newspapers or in any magazines but company-sponsored publications. Reviewers hired by the Web sites are working for booksellers whose primary interest lies not in literary criticism but in selling books, and to say there's a conflict of interest is an understatement. Not surprisingly these reviewers find much to praise and little to criticize in the books they review; indeed, even though selection at these Web sites is linked to high sales figures rather than quality (books with negligible sales for the most part go unreviewed), negative reviews are hard to find. The brief reviews tend to read like write-ups from the publisher, a reminder that we're one click away from a sale.

Reader-reviewers, of course, aren't hired by the booksellers. Anyone can write a review and within certain general guidelines (no obscenity, for example) can express whatever opinions they wish. But this army of volunteers, it seems to me, is nonetheless working for the booksellers, enhancing their Web pages with commentary that might stir up interest and help sell books. Barnes and Noble claims the copyright to these reviews, which "become the sole property of Barnes & Noble.com." Amazon has actively involved itself in its reader forum and influenced its transformation into a new kind of reviewing medium.

Having found a workforce willing to review at no cost, Amazon has shrewdly nurtured it. Although the company may not individually solicit, screen, edit, or pay reviewers, it does encourage them with a system of rewards. For one thing, it has developed a status system, in which it awards reviewers a "reviewer rank," which is determined by the number of "helpful" votes reviewers receive from readers who can vote on any review they read. "Top Reviewers" in this list are rewarded with publicity: each is identified as a "Top Reviewer" in each review he or she writes; they're featured, jointly, on a "Top Reviewers" page, in which they appear in rank order, each receiving a contributor's bio, and, if he or she chooses, a picture. Second, Amazon allows space for all reviewers to provide biographical information in its "see more about me" feature. Third, it "spotlights" certain reviews, which are lifted out of the chronological order in which reviews usually appear to the top of the page and headlined "spotlight reviews," becoming essentially what in print media would be a lead review.

That these techniques have been successful in luring reviewers is evident in the emergence of a group of reviewers who seem to be making careers out of reviewing for Amazon. Two of the "Top Reviewers" have reviewed more than 6,500 books each. That Amazon, increasingly visited and visible, has gained clout is evident in the fact that its top reviewers now receive galleys and books from authors and publishers, who hope they will review them.

"Let's hear it for democracy!" says Amazon. And to be sure this is democracy at work. But Amazon has created a system that not only allows but encourages ethical and literary standards far lower than those we find in print reviewing. To begin with, because Amazon neither solicits nor screens reviewers and allows them to remain anonymous, reviewers have the option of being dishonest. Many seize the opportunity. When Amazon's Canadian Web site went wonky one week in 2004, exposing the names of anonymous reviewers, authors were revealed to have reviewed their own books, promoted the books of friends, and attacked more prominent authors they thought overrated. I can't imagine that many people were surprised by these revelations, which I have assumed to be common knowledge for a very long time. But the problem isn't only that an author's mother or a rival feels free to "review" a book, as, of course, each does. Or that friends of the author may feel compelled to counteract negative reviews. Reader-reviewers pay attention to any number of extraliterary considerations. When, for example, Jonathan Franzen expressed qualms about having his novel *The Corrections* associated with Oprah Winfrey's Book Club, and Oprah withdrew her invitation for him to appear on her television show, some of her many fans proceeded to attack the novel on Amazon in the guise of reviewing it.

If anonymous self-publication paves the way for dishonesty, the reviewer-ranking system encourages it: reviewers competing to improve their ranking can easily ask friends to cast "helpful" votes for their reviews and rise for reasons entirely unrelated to the quality of their critiques. That quality isn't improved by the fact that the more reviews reviewers write the more helpful votes they may receive, which encourages speedy reading and sloppy writing (6,500 reviews!). And while reviewers are free to be as unfavorable as they please, and many do pan books, reviews that praise have a better chance of being "spotlighted": out of 32 spotlight reviews chosen at random, 20 5-star ratings and 5 with 4 stars hardly constitute a strong critical showing. Finally, since Amazon doesn't screen reviewers for qualifications or edit their contributions, reviewers do not necessarily feel required to know about a subject or even the basics of good writing. As you would expect, many of the reviews are ignorant and abominably written. "The FROG KING"—concludes a review written by Amazon's Top Reviewer, which won 6 out of 9 "helpful" votes—

> is an amusing Manhattan romp starring a goofball, whom the intelligent Evie should have earlier or better yet, never take up with such a dud in the first place. The story line is jocularly satirical when Adam Davies takes the reader inside the nastiest elements of the publishing industry as seen from someone enviously looking up at the butts that he wants working exclusively on his manuscript. However, the tale loses steam after awhile as most of the plot centers on the aptly named FROG KING, a buffoon who spends too more time riveted on his needs than forging a meaningful relationship.[10]

Whatever our complaints about print criticism, it's hard to imagine a newspaper or magazine publishing a review like that; yet Amazon honors the reviewer.

The quality of reviews on Amazon suggests the importance in traditional publications of book page editors, middlemen—and women—in the review process. If reviews are inevitably influenced by the newspapers and magazines they're written for, reviewers absorb that influence partly by reading the publications and partly through review editors who are answerable at larger enterprises to their own editors and publishers, accountable for the conception of the book page, endowed with their own taste and personalities, and directly in touch with reviewers. Whatever the character of any particular editor-reviewer relationship, which is inherently personal as well as professional, it is one a reviewer can't ignore. It's the editor who hires the reviewer, who accepts or rejects his work, and who provides him with or deprives him of regular assignments. It's the editor who bestows or withholds the praise that reviewers, like all writers, need and aren't likely otherwise to get since readers seldom send in letters praising reviewers; if they write at all, it's usually to complain. It's the editor who, by talking to reviewers about books, makes them feel part of the literary world, who makes them feel like writers.

From the perspective of the reviewer, who both wants and needs to please the editor, the editor is in a position of power, which she can wield for better or worse. Editors, who are often themselves reviewers, understand the reviewer's work and can be sympathetic to its peculiar complexities; aware of how little they pay reviewers, they may feel compassionate as well. But the relationship can lead to impatience: from the editor's perspective, reviewers have little understanding of the obligations involved in running a book page, have little sense of the larger page outside their single review, and are often narcissistically unaware that she has a dozen other reviewers to deal with. And power can of course breed arrogance. I have worked with some highhanded editors, though never one quite as highhanded as George A. Woods, former editor for children's books at the *New York Times Book Review,* who declared, in an essay written for potential reviewers:

> If I ask for 200 words, I guarantee that these will be some of the hardest 200 words that person has ever produced. You may be asked to rewrite, to clarify, to point up; you may be asked "what do you mean by this phrase or that line," either on the telephone or in a letter. Or you may not hear from me for several months and, being too terrified to contact me because I am awesome and formidable, imagine that you have failed dismally. And then one day, lo and behold, there is your work in print. O frabjous day. But just because you have been printed once does not make it certain that you will be printed again. Attribute it to my whimsicality, business, forgetfulness or that you caused me too much trouble in the editing. On the other hand, you may receive another book to review in a few months. Nothing is certain, and I am under no obligation to anyone—editor, author, artist, review writer—only to the child.[11]

Such overt flaunting of power is not, in my experience, typical of review editors. Perhaps being review editor for children's books, a field unfairly lacking in status, got to Mr. Woods, and he needed to pass the contempt on to those on the next rung down; or perhaps the status of the *Times* went to his head. But it seems to me that in this statement he makes explicit what generally underlies the editor-reviewer relationship: it's the editor who holds the ultimate power of publication, the editor who needs to be pleased. And just as a respectful editor can give a reviewer backbone, a demeaning editor like Woods can undermine confidence, making a reviewer so fearful of what he should or shouldn't say, he grows more concerned about pleasing the editor than doing justice to the book.

Editors convey their preferences in a variety of subtle and not-so-subtle ways: by what they ask for and how they ask for it, by what they praise—in books and reviews—and what they disparage, by what they edit in or out, by the kind of reviews and reviewers they publish. This pertains not only to such issues as clarity, prose, emphasis, or the use of quotations, but also to the kinds of assessments they want, in general and for particular books. Some editors will encourage specific judgments, most will respect the reviewer's right to independent opinion. But the editor who regularly publishes the "hatchet jobs" of Dale Peck is making one statement, while the editor who regularly publishes the work of the reviewer who never met a book he didn't like is making another. The editor who assigns a long review of an author whom he tells the reviewer he thinks is "brilliant" or "overrated" has set the stage for the review that he wants. And the editor who, in reprinting one of my columns, neatly excised the paragraph that contained my criticism may have done so, as she claimed, for "space," but since she left my praise intact she sent a clear message: she found criticism dispensable (and undesirable).

Realistically, it makes sense that most editors would prefer favorable reviews. They justify the space devoted to books, are more likely to be read by readers looking for recommendations, and are healthy for relationships with book publishers as well as with editors' own editors and publishers. And as a reviewer, I've generally felt that when I've liked a book, editors have been pleased for *me*, glad that the assignment turned out to be a positive, if not a lucrative, experience. This isn't to say that editors will encourage reviewers to be dishonest, though they sometimes do. But reviewers can't help but be aware that editors prefer the praise that is a feel-good experience for everyone involved.

Indeed, most of the pressures exerted on the reviewer as he sits alone in his study move reviews in the direction of praise. This is obviously true of that exerted by publishers, who of course shouldn't be a source of pressure, who shouldn't be in the room at all. From the reviewer's viewpoint, after all, reviews are criticism, but from the publisher's, they're promotion; almost all review business, from sending out galleys to collecting clips, is handled by the publicity department, whose aim is to get as many reviews as possible and use what influence it can to make these reviews favorable. Review editors, by tradition, try to keep reviewers and publicists apart, handling all correspondence with publishers themselves.

But the publisher enters the room nonetheless. To begin with, experienced reviewers, like review editors, are aware of publishing houses, which they identify with particular kinds of books and which can influence their opinions. If a book is from a highly respected house, say, Knopf, they will approach it expecting a certain quality, which will increase the chances that they'll find it, and if their initial impression is that the book is truly poor, they may wonder whether perhaps they're wrong, whether perhaps they didn't "get" it, and they may end up tempering their criticism. In the case of small press books, I've heard reviewers wonder whether, with small presses struggling for survival, they should contribute to their downfall with a negative review, and again they may temper their criticism.

And then publishers also make their presence felt through the material they send: the press releases, the media kits, the galleys. Unless the reviewer is scrupulous, he can be influenced by the sizable print run, the substantial publicity, the important endorsements, all of which tell him the book will be big, it will be noticed, which may lead him to wonder what other reviewers will say. Even the publisher's description of a book can affect a reviewer's conception of it, and the reviewer who reads the press release will be on the way to reading the book the way the publisher wants him to read it.

Finally, although publishers can't easily buy praise, they can reward it. By extracting blurbs from favorable reviews and using them in advertising for the book as well as on the covers of future editions and paperbacks, publishers boost reviewers: reviewers win points with publications, which are always identified in the blurbs and which enjoy the prestige and free publicity; and they win points with review editors, whose undervalued book pages get credit. My editors certainly took notice if my reviews were quoted and would pass the news on to me. Blurbs are part of the little recognition reviewers get in the world, and though in recent years some stylish presses have actually cited negative reviews for promotion, blurbs are awarded, for the most part, only for praise.

The author too exerts pressure toward favorable coverage; though only his book should be in the reviewer's study, his presence may be felt. Reviewers know that to be fair they should focus only on the text, which they should read, respond to, and evaluate with as much detachment as they can muster.

But when the reviewer opens the book mailer, there is the author. His name is on the book jacket. Reviewers can't pretend they've never heard of Saul Bellow or Margaret Atwood. If the name is unfamiliar, publishers, who have no desire for detached reviewing, do their best to introduce the author: they send along a photograph, a press release with biographical information ("She grew up on a farm in Iowa," "He drove a cab in New York City"), personal essays ("Why I Write," "An Interview with Myself"), a list of prizes the author has won and the prestigious magazines in which his work has previously appeared, which, if they're sufficiently prestigious, may predispose a reviewer to think highly of the author or, later, make him doubt his own negative opinion of the book.

It's hard to prevent the author from becoming an extraliterary presence. Most reviewers, by convention, will be kind to a first effort, unwilling to crush new talent. Timid reviewers may be intimidated by a reputation. Loyal reviewers may not want to denigrate the work of a beloved author. And we read a book differently when it's written by someone whose work we know, whose literary worldview is familiar: the flaws themselves become interesting. Determined to be fair to book and author, it's easy to forget about being fair (i.e., honest) to the reader.

You might think that the reviewer who kept readers most firmly in mind would be the most honest, the most inclined to tell the truth about a book, good or bad. But at partisan publications, reviewers will be expected by readers to write partisan reviews. At general-interest publications, reviewers trying to appeal to a broad spectrum of readers may focus so intently on being entertaining that they'll make a book seem more interesting than it is. Suspecting that many readers will, as the review editor fears, simply skip an essentially negative review, as they intend to skip the book, reviewers may also make the book seem better than it is.

And reviewers too focused on imagining their readers may find themselves reflecting that most readers don't necessarily have high critical standards. Readers may be quite particular about what they read, but the bestsellers and most popular books aren't generally the literary fiction and serious nonfiction most reviewers might consider the best. In making my assessments, then, is it my role to guide readers to the kinds of books I like or the kinds of books they like? The book reviewer's task may not be as difficult as that of the movie reviewer, who is forced to review blockbuster films, no matter how schlocky, just because they're playing and who knows beforehand that whatever he says, they will most likely be box office hits: many book pages choose to ignore badly written bestsellers. But in our age of cultural relativism, when the notion of objective authority in all critical judgments has been questioned, I think all reviewers are forced to ask themselves whether they're improving taste or merely imposing their own.

In the midst of all of this, reviewers face professional dilemmas of their own. If they entered the field with high standards, as most of us did, the reality of reviewing comes as a blow. For one thing, as George Orwell pointed out, the first thing reviewers will need to do is lower their standards. Their own favorite authors may be Tolstoy or Austen, but they won't be reviewing the works of Tolstoy or Austen; rather they will see books that are mostly far inferior, and "it is no use monotonously saying, of book after book, 'This book is tripe.'" They will have to "discover something which is *not* tripe, and pretty frequently, or get the sack."[12]

For another, few publications these days are looking for pointed criticism, and the reviewer who wants to write it will have to compete for the few spots available. More publications, I've found, especially newspapers and especially for fiction, want enthusiasm. Enthusiasm for the field, of course, is crucial for all reviewing: the critic who is bored with books, or movies, or dance, or who feels his work doesn't matter shouldn't be reviewing. But what we need is the enthusiasm of engagement, not of cheerleading. Editors rightly want reviewers who "love" books, which should mean they want critics who love books so much they hold them to high standards, but it tends to mean the opposite: they want critics who love books so much they can always find something good to say about them. The reviewer who praises will never be out of work.

American reviewers who are persistently critical will find that they're writing against the cultural grain. Ours is a culture that generally doesn't welcome criticism—a culture in which we tend to feel that criticism is impolite, that it's in bad taste, that, as the saying goes, if you have nothing good to say, you shouldn't say anything at all; a culture in which one certainly shouldn't get too worked up about bad writing: "I have long felt that any reviewer who expresses rage and loathing for a novel is preposterous," said Kurt Vonnegut. "He or she is like a person who has put on full armor and attacked a hot fudge sundae or a banana split."[13] Audiences are happy to have a book club leader, preferably Oprah, recommend a book absolutely, but they don't demand that she analyze its flaws, and I strongly doubt they want her to discuss books that she thinks reflect negative trends in fiction. As John Maxwell Hamilton observed in his essay on book reviewing, appropriately titled "Inglorious Employment," Oprah has not been a critic but "a book cheerleader," and this has been what her fans have enjoyed.[14] In America it sometimes seems that *de libris*—as *de mortuis*—*nil nisi bonum.*

With so many factors discouraging criticism, it takes courage and confidence for a reviewer to go his own way and tell readers that the latest "masterpiece" isn't very good. Amid the waves of praise, he risks not only what all critics risk, being wrong, but being wrong alone. In retrospect, I stand by my negative reviews, but I recall with real regret those reviews in which I praised books I didn't think were very good, not out of laziness, or friendship with the author, or even generosity, but out of weakness, an inability to combat the pressures. In "Crisis in Critville," Dwight Garner proposed "a new rule": "Critics may only praise books they're willing to force their friends to read."[15] This seems a good path to honesty, yet I doubt reviewers could ever clear this road on their own. Certainly, the burden falls on reviewers: they alone are aware of the degree to which they have been honest. But reviewers figure low in the hierarchy of reviewing and lack the power to effect this change. Unless publications and editors support serious criticism—discriminating criticism—reviewers will often opt for finding what is good in a book or devoting their space, dully, to description and offering as few judgments as possible. They will end up giving the impression that books are far better than they think they are, though in private, should you run into them at a party, they may give you the critical reading that never quite made it into print.

Are Book Reviews Necessary?

The history of criticism begins with the history of art. When the first artist drew his first horse in red chalk on the walls of his cave, the first critic was at his elbow. And as the other cave dwellers gathered to see and wonder, he doubtless diverted their attention from the artist and his work to himself by raising the pregnant question, "What is criticism, and what is its function at the present time?"

—Robert Morss Lovett, "Criticism: Past and Present," *New Republic,* October 26, 1921

. . . we might remind ourselves that criticism is as inevitable as breathing, and that we should be none the worse for articulating what passes in our minds when we read a book and feel an emotion about it, for criticizing our own minds in their work of criticism.

—T. S. Eliot, "Tradition and the Individual Talent"

In recent years, book reviewing seems to have added new dimensions to its perpetual decline. As many newspapers across the country trimmed their book pages in the past decade, the familiar lament about the declining quality of reviews was joined by a lament about their declining number. "Those Dying Book Reviews," ran a headline on Pat Holt's online newsletter "Holt Uncensored." "The Incredible Vanishing Book Review," ran the headline of an article on *Salon.* The declining power of reviews came into play as well. "Everyone says reviews are less and less important in selling books," said the editor Jonathan Galassi, of Farrar, Straus and Giroux, in a *Harvard Magazine* profile in 1997.

Indeed, the former head of Book Sense, an organization of independent bookstores, suggested that "traditional" reviews might well be destined for extinction, replaced by alternative kinds of book coverage.[1]

It strikes me as a little early to write off traditional book reviewing, if by "traditional" we mean the process of editorial oversight, from the selection of books and reviewers to the approval of copy, a process that works equally in print and online media. Print reviews are still numerous: Publishers Marketplace, a publishing Web site, has in the past few years compiled an index of more than thirty thousand reviews. For prestige, our major print review media have yet to be surpassed. And publications, both print and electronic, now offer traditional reviews online.

Nonetheless, it's certainly true that as traditional reviews in print media have been shrinking in number, alternative sources of book information, commentary, and recommendations have been multiplying. The Web, of course, has opened up a vast field of coverage for books as it has for all arts journalism. Two bookselling Web sites offer full catalogs, with publishing data, book descriptions, excerpts, author self-interviews, customized recommendations, specialized lists, ads, plus their own and readers' reviews. Book Sense offers its own choice of noteworthy books—the Book Sense Picks and Book Sense Notables—all accompanied by bookseller write-ups, available through the Web sites of independent bookstores as well as its own. Online book sites provide news, interviews, discussions, and blogs. Individual bookstores, authors, publishers, and commentators have Web sites and blogs of their own. But the Web has accounted for only part of this expanding coverage. Both chain and independent bookstores as well as libraries schedule numerous readings and book signings. Print and electronic media offer author profiles and interviews. Television programs and book clubs spotlight authors and their books. A great many books now include readers' guides designed for reading groups. And reading groups are visited by authors, who answer questions about their books.

This is an extraordinary amount of book coverage, surely more than we have ever had before, and the sheer mass of it raises the question of whether we need reviews as well. After all, reviews have been causing dissatisfaction for two hundred years. If they are disappearing, would it be such a bad thing if we just allowed them to vanish? Isn't it possible that these many alternatives can better serve publishers and authors, readers and books themselves?

Publishers apparently seem to think they might. When newspapers, suffering financial problems, reduced their book pages, many critics took them to task for their bottom-line approach to journalism. But the more striking issue, it seems to me, is that book publishers let it happen. I doubt after all that newspapers would have cut their book sections had book advertising been forthcoming. Yet publishers, even faced with the loss of reviews, withheld their support. A variety of factors were involved, as always, including book publishers' own hard times. But in failing to support reviews with even a minimum of advertising, publishers sent an implicit message: book reviews are expendable.

Publishers have long been ambivalent about the value of advertising, wary of its cost, and dubious about its effectiveness. It's widely believed in the field that in most cases ads do not sell books, and that it's only when a book is already selling that an ad will be of real use. As the English publisher Sir Stanley Unwin memorably argued in his classic, *The Truth about Publishing*, and again in 1938 in *Best-Sellers: Are They Born or Made?* "It is as a reminder that book advertising is most effective. Just as whipping will maintain, and even accelerate, the speed of a top that is already spinning, but will achieve nothing with one lying dormant on the ground, so advertising will maintain and even accelerate the sales of a book which is already being talked about, but will do little or nothing for one in which there is otherwise no interest."[2] Thus, while the general public—and authors—may think, as they look at the full-page color ads for best-selling books by Danielle Steel or Mary Higgins Clark, "No wonder they sell so well. If serious fiction—my book!—received those ads, it too would sell well," according to Unwin this isn't the case. Advertising did not create these bestsellers, it followed sales and helped to "whip the top"; for books that aren't already selling, advertising would not generate enough sales to pay for itself.

Publishers do of course advertise books that aren't bestsellers, but when they take out these ads—which are generally neither full-page nor in color—they often do so for reasons other than selling books: they may advertise to maintain a public presence, to satisfy the egos of important authors, to impress authors they want to lure away from other publishers, to support booksellers. For Unwin, one of these subsidiary reasons was to support reviews. His own firm, he said, advertised consistently in the political and literary weeklies.

> Papers like the *Times Literary Supplement* could not exist without the support of publishers; it is doubtful whether the political weeklies could do so. It is certain that daily papers such as the *Daily Telegraph* and the *News Chronicle,* not to mention the provincial press, the importance of which is so often underestimated, could or would not continue to devote the space they do to the review of current literature were they deprived of all book advertisements.[3]

Moreover, he argued, to concentrate all advertising in the Sunday papers would not only lose the benefit of reviews in "many directions," which would disappear, but would also drive up the cost of advertising in the favored few. This, it seems to me, is pretty much what has happened here, where trade publishers' failure to advertise in the opinion magazines, in the provincial newspapers, and in the review magazines has helped to dry up reviews in these "many directions"—and caused literary magazines to fold—while their decision to put so much of their advertising in the *New York Times Book Review* has indeed driven up its cost, depleting the budget that remains for ads in other places.

Clearly, Unwin's appreciation of reviews has not been entirely shared by American publishers, who historically have expressed a wide range of attitudes on the subject, depending on the nature of their lists and their personal views. In 1923, in *A Publisher's Confession,* Walter Hines Page dismissed reviews entirely: "I, for one, and I know no publisher who holds a different opinion, care nothing for the judgment of the professional literary class," he said, claiming that reviews of novels, for example, had neither permanent value nor impact on sales and that he viewed them only as "so much publicity." Other early publishers saw more merit in that publicity. J. C. Derby, in his memoir, *Fifty Years among Authors, Books and Publishers,* pays attention to the impact of reviews on sales, noting at one point of Victor Hugo's *Les Misérables,* "The sale was not large at first, but the newspaper critics soon made it popular." As Donald Sheehan observes in *This Was Publishing,* two *Publishers Weekly* polls early in the century revealed that publishers acknowledged the commercial value of reviews, and "it was reported, in contradiction to Walter Page's assertion, that George

Brett, the president of The Macmillan Company, made every effort to see the reviews of all the books submitted."[4]

In 1997, when Marie Arana-Ward, then deputy editor of the *Washington Post Book World,* asked publishers their opinion of reviewing, she got just the mixed response you would expect. While a publisher of potential bestsellers, books that don't depend upon reviews to sell and have not traditionally been reviewed, called reviews "a negative culture" and said she didn't read them, a publisher of midlist books—that is, serious nonfiction and literary fiction—said, "For an editor like me . . . print reviews are lifeblood."[5] In Dan Moldea's libel suit against the *New York Times* in 1994, publishers seemed to rally to the cause of reviewing; according to the *Times,* the Association of American Publishers joined in filing a brief asserting that "Personal interpretation of literary works is the essence of readership and of literary criticism."[6]

But whatever American publishers may have said about reviewing, on the whole they've been only selectively supportive, helpful to a few prominent publications and offering little assistance to the rest. When I was editor of *New Boston Review,* a small literary arts magazine devoted largely to books, I had trouble persuading even Boston-based publishers—including, at the time, Houghton Mifflin and Little, Brown—that it was worth their while to advertise. The *Boston Globe* today, like many newspapers, receives little publisher advertising, despite a sizable book section and circulation. But this lack of publisher support is evident not only in publishers' reluctance to advertise heavily in provincial papers and opinion magazines but even more fundamentally, as we've seen, in their negligence in getting review copies of books to literary editors around the country—their failure even to send books of regional relevance to editors in the region. Editors can't review books they don't have, and publishers, by making it so difficult to obtain them, have made it clear that they don't care whether or not they do.

Of course, publishers have some reason to feel ambivalent about reviews, which may praise their products but can trash them as well. People in the publishing field like to say that even bad publicity is good, but while a negative review may be better than no review, nobody really wants their product knocked. The publisher, however much a middleman producing rather than writing a book, has selected the book, assessed it as valuable, overseen its production, and paid its passage into the world. A trashing is a personal insult that reflects on the publisher's taste and business judgment. Why support publicity that is denigrating, why pay to be judged a fool? More to the point, perhaps—though I believe the personal element shouldn't be underestimated in what is very much a personal field—if negative reviews harm sales, they inflict financial damage. Why support an enterprise that may harm their own and, many publishers believe, do little to help.

From a sales perspective, publishers have never been certain how much influence reviews have, for better or worse. They know that reviews in the trade magazines have an enormous impact on bookstore orders and library purchases. They know that a review in the major review media, most notably the *New York Times Book Review,* will have an effect, both directly and in its repercussions, leading not only to other reviews, but also to interviews, profiles, and television appearances, or, if negative, to the cancellation of any already scheduled. Research on book-buying habits has generally indicated that consumers do use reviews in choosing books. In a survey commissioned by *Publishers Weekly* and BookExpo America in 1999, for example, three hundred booksellers, half independents and half chain stores, included reviews both in the *New York Times Book Review* and in local papers as influencing book buyers' choices. A 2002 *Publishers Weekly* article linked reviews in several major newspapers directly to sales.[7]

But publishing is not a field that has relied heavily on such research, which has tended to be sporadic and not exactly scientific. This may change as methods of tracking book sales become increasingly precise. But realistically the impact of reviews is hard to measure. Publishers and authors are doing many kinds of promotion simultaneously, which makes it difficult to sort out the influence of any one effort. If an author on a book tour in Chicago has given six readings, has been profiled in one newspaper and reviewed in another, who can say with any certainty, should his book sales rise, what role was played by the review? Moreover, it's impossible to generalize about the impact of reviews when that impact is so variable and unreliable: every year some books that get excellent reviews in prominent publications inexplicably do not sell especially well, while some books ignored by the major media do.

Why a book sells in any quantity has always been something of a mystery. Though publishers today probably wouldn't express it quite as enigmatically as Robert Sterling Yard did almost a century ago, declaring, "It is the Book Itself that Sells Itself," nonetheless they know that the book trade can never be entirely predictable, and that they are to some degree gamblers. Risk is so intrinsic to publishing, it's surely part of its appeal as a profession. The unpredictability relates mainly to new books by unknown or little-known authors—but not to these alone. Writing about *Elegy for Iris,* John Bayley's memoir about his experiences with his wife, Iris Murdoch, who was suffering from Alzheimer's disease, the editor Robert Weil, who commissioned the book, said that the "advance had been so modest, and the subject supposedly so grim, that no one could imagine that the book would go on to become both a national bestseller and the basis for an Oscar-winning movie."[8]

Every year *Publishers Weekly* runs a survey of bookselling successes and failures, "The Red and the Black," that reveals how books defy the expectations of the canniest and most experienced of publishers. Publishers can speculate after the fact on why readers took up one book and ignored another that seemed equally good—or bad—and equally favored by publisher promotion and press reviews, but they know that all things are not equal in the book field, that every product is different, and that their speculations are of limited use both for understanding the fate of a particular book and for applying the experience to any future book.

"It is unsafe to be dogmatic about the reasons for the success of any book, because nothing can ever be proved," wrote Michael Joseph, in *The Adventure of Publishing.*

> The time of publication, the competition with which it is faced, the prevalent mood of the reading public (which can change very quickly) these and many other factors contribute to the success or failure of any book. It is never possible to repeat the conditions in which a particular book has been published. We can only guess how much influence is exercised by reviews and advertising.[9]

What everyone seems to agree upon is that it's word-of-mouth that sells books: friends telling friends, talk, "buzz." The unknowable factor is what sets this in motion. Sometimes a review can achieve it, becoming what one publicist has called a "selling review," which she described as " . . . a review that people might talk about," a review that "goes beyond appearing in print" and "becomes part of conversation." Most editors can cite cases where such reviews helped create bestsellers. Arana-Ward has pointed to Jonathan Yardley's review of John Berendt's *Midnight in the Garden of Good and Evil,* which appeared in the *Washington Post Book World,* and John Updike's review of Erica Jong's *Fear of Flying,* which appeared in the *New Yorker.* At a 1998 National Arts Journalism Program symposium on publishing, the editor William B. Strachan remarked that when he was at Viking, reviews of William Kennedy's new work "pushed sales from three thousand copies to best-sellerdom." In an article on "The Power of Print Media," *Publishers Weekly* cited a *New York Times Book Review* cover review by Francine Prose of Jonathan Safran Foer's *Everything Is Illuminated* as pushing the book "over the top."[10]

But instances of this have never been common and usually depend on the publication being prominent and the reviewer well known, respected, and trusted—which is one reason that publishers have remained willing to advertise in major publications while neglecting even to send review copies to "minor" ones. A rave from Ms. Unknown Reviewer in the *Small Town Record* won't do it. But even rave reviews in prominent publications often don't do it, and, as Galassi and others in the field have suggested, in recent years they seem to be doing it with diminishing frequency.

In view of the unmeasurable, unreliable, potentially negative, and apparently limited value of reviews for selling books, I find it easy to see why publishers have welcomed other kinds of book coverage. For publishers already skeptical about the audience for traditional book reviews, which have never had the alleged power of theater reviews to make or break a play, nontraditional coverage in print and at online book sites and even the reader-reviews on our popular bookselling sites present a new way of reaching readers and may seem no worse than the traditional reviews that many perceive as a shoddy product. For generating word-of-mouth recommendations, book reviews can't compete with appearances on popular television and radio shows, which reach audiences that are vast in comparison with print circulations and which, along with profiles, interviews, book clubs, and readings, create an element of personal interest that is better suited to our personality-oriented times than literary criticism and easier to absorb. For publishers of genre, the many online sites devoted to romance, science fiction, and mystery bring attention to books often shunted to the back or ignored altogether in mainstream reviewing.

And, of course, most of the alternative coverage isn't critical. Booksellers are as eager as publishers to sell books, and most of the information they provide—whether in newsletters or Book Sense "reviews"—is favorable. Author interviews and profiles, whether live or in print, are seldom critical. Whether they are personality pieces or more literary interviews, these features, much like the movie celebrity features that run on newspaper arts and entertainment pages, focus more on the people than on the work, and they are carried out in cooperation with the author by reporters who usually work from the assumption that their role is to celebrate the author rather than to challenge or criticize his work. At newspapers, these pieces are often handled by the review editor who, by convention, refrains from being critical: even if he loathes the author's book, he leaves the criticism to the review that will follow and keeps his tone positive, sending the message that the author is worth noting and so, by implication, is the book. Book clubs, too, provide praise for the fortunate books they select. Online reviews on book-reviewing Web sites can be negative, but partaking as they do of the Web's egalitarian aura, in which every opinion is considered no more than an individual's view and is often prefaced by IMHO ("In My Humble Opinion"), many of these sites accentuate, even insist upon, the positive. Mainly, it's the reader-reviews on the bookselling sites that are potentially as negative as traditional reviews.

Clearly, these various kinds of coverage can be useful to publishers, in some cases more useful than reviews. But in my not-so-humble opinion, they serve publishers poorly as a substitute for reviewing. Substantial book sections—which might be published online, of course—offer publishers the best chance of getting attention for the largest number of their books. While a single issue of a large book section can review dozens of books—and could cover more with additional advertising support—interviews, profiles, and readings provide room for one discussion at a time, and as media formats they aren't expandable. To cover a greater number of books, more interviews, profiles, and readings would need to be scheduled. But neither television nor radio would be interested in running author interviews twenty-four hours a day; there isn't enough audience. Bookstores and libraries can only arrange a certain number of readings;

they have other business to attend to and, again, as many sparsely attend-
ed readings make clear, a limited audience. And while it's obvious that no
review can have the sales impact of a beloved television celebrity like
Oprah recommending a book she loves to an audience of millions, hoping for this sort of thing to happen is, as many people have noted, like hoping to win the lottery. It would be far better for publishers to support the
print equivalents of Oprah, the prominent, trusted columnists whose recommendations readers value and who are a rarity now in newspapers
which, bereft of advertising, have mostly abandoned them.

While certain kinds of books don't need reviews to sell, others depend
on them. A book by a major or best-selling author—Philip Roth or John
Grisham—has a large ready-made audience who will buy it as soon as it
appears; all the publisher has to do is announce these books, then run ads
as they begin to sell: the publisher's task is simply to let people know
they're available. But this is hardly the case with books by new or little-
known authors, who have no readers eagerly awaiting their work. Nor is
it the case with most serious nonfiction and literary fiction, midlist books
that may be neither topical nor sexy and need some kind of explication to
find an audience.

Authors of such books aren't likely to be invited to appear on television
shows that depend upon using writers or subjects guaranteed to attract
mass audiences. They will face steep competition for radio interviews.
They will not be profiled or interviewed in print unless they have some interesting personal story to tell. They will have to compete for the coveted
reading slots at bookstores and libraries, which, though they may not pay,
have enough options to be quite selective in their choices and tend to prefer authors who are sufficiently well known and respected that they will
draw an audience. Nor are they even likely to be reviewed on the bookselling Web sites: Amazon and Barnes and Noble reviewers themselves
review the books that don't need reviews—again, Philip Roth or John
Grisham—and most reader-reviewers do as well. Only for "big" books are
there hundreds of reader-reviews; for small books there are usually few,
and most people suspect that these are written by friends and relatives and
can't be trusted.

For publishers, uncritical book "features" may seem preferable to reviews. But a steady stream of approbation is not only cloying, it fails to
persuade—as is already evident from our overadulatory reviewing: puff

pieces with no critical counterweight lose credibility. Moreover, it's ultimately ineffective, leaving even readers who believe it unable to choose between one "fascinating" book and another.

In any case, although reviews, from the publisher's viewpoint, are promotion, to assess them solely by their sales value seems to me misguided.
Selling books isn't actually the goal of a review. Indeed, once reviews are
judged "good" because they lead to many sales, or "bad" because they fail
to sell, the values for reviewing get distorted. Bad reviews, after all, can sell
books but they're nonetheless bad reviews: a review that misrepresents a
book and gives it more praise than the reviewer thinks it really deserves
may sell copies but it's hardly a good review. Conversely, a review that dis-
sects the illogical argument at the center of a book on politics may be an
excellent review, though it may not encourage sales.

Even viewed as a consumer's guide, a book page is not about buying; reviews are about reading. The reviewer may recommend a particular book,
but he has nothing to say about whether the reader takes it out of the library, borrows it from a friend, or buys it. The reviewer needs to be per-
suasive in arguing why the book succeeds or fails, but what he is selling is
a viewpoint not a book. He is presumably a skilled reader, someone who
has specialized in reading, and his review is an explication—an explana-
tion, clarification, interpretation—of his experience of reading a particular book. If it's a good review, it's also about the experience of reading,
which is rendered interesting.

Uncritical features that focus on authors and topics do not in themselves make *reading* interesting, and I question whether the alternatives to
reviews that are popping up are building an audience of readers. A 2003
feature in *Publishers Weekly,* "The Hunt for New Readers," provided some
disturbing statistics on American reading: "According to Veronis Suhler
Stevenson's most recent *Communications Industry Forecast,* the time
Americans spent reading a book fell from 123 hours per year in 1996 to
109 hours in 2001. Even other print media fared better." And according to
research from Ipsos-NPD, "the number of households buying at least one
book per year has dropped steadily over the last five years, falling from
60% to 56.5% in 2001."[11] That these declines have occurred while the
amount of book coverage—apart from reviews—has been rising suggests
that that coverage isn't helping to create either the readers or the book
buyers that publishers need. Publishers might think hard about whether

good reviews might better serve their books, authors, and economic future.

Authors, of course, even more than publishers, have good reason to feel ambivalent about reviews. Whatever the publisher may suffer from a negative review, for authors it can be devastating. Book reviewers at least don't generally deride an author's appearance, as film, theater, and dance critics sometimes do—though the review may be accompanied by a less-than-flattering caricature of the author: Katha Pollitt, in a *New York Times* op-ed piece about a bad review, "Thank You for Hating My Book," lamented that the drawing of her made her look like "a demented chicken." But the criticism feels personal, it's humiliating, and they have no recourse; the letter to the editor they know they shouldn't send—what Paul Fussell has called the "A.B.M.," or Author's Big Mistake—makes them sound wounded, not right.[12] Can they *prove* that their novel was not a pack of sentimental drivel, that it wouldn't have been better to spare the trees? The legend that a bad review was the cause of Keats's death may be apocryphal, but like most such tales it holds its kernel of truth. We have no way of knowing the impact of nasty reviews on writers who may not have died but did stop writing as a consequence, another form of death. So negatively did Virginia Woolf feel about reviews—at least, reviews of "imaginative" literature: poetry, drama, and fiction—that in her essay "Reviewing," she suggested eliminating these altogether and publishing only reviews of nonfiction, which she considered to be useful.

Yet whatever authors may suffer from reviews, with their drawbacks and inflicted pain, I don't believe that even authors of imaginative literature would be better off in a literary world without them. Whether Woolf's own proposal—that authors work with private consultants who would serve as personal critics and that editors replace reviews with long critical essays—might improve literature is debatable. But as Leonard Woolf observed in the "Note" that he appended to his wife's essay, her system wouldn't help readers select books, which is a central purpose of reviewing. Perhaps the author spared reviews wouldn't be discouraged from her work; perhaps her work would even be improved, but who would know about that work and who would read it?

If some authors don't need reviews, many would fare badly if they were forced to depend solely on our contemporary alternatives, with their own drawbacks and inflicted pain. Television appearances, radio shows, interviews, profiles, and readings do not favor the writer who is neither photogenic nor telegenic, who is not a dynamic or even a comfortable public speaker, who has not had an especially intriguing, unusual life or who is reticent by nature. Such writers might find themselves without promotional opportunities, and the quality of their books wouldn't necessarily matter. Writers may be frustrated by reviewers who, even when they write favorable reviews, don't "get" their books—but would it be less frustrating to depend solely on interviewers who, as is often the case, haven't even read them? Writers may find their egos demeaned by critical assessments of their work. But are their egos boosted by having to beg for readings from booksellers who are weighing their importance and popularity? Does their confidence rise when, should they be granted those readings, only a handful of people—or none at all—show up? And should they find their work solely in the hands of a reader-reviewer on Amazon whose semicomprehensible comments accompany a poor rating of a single star—which shines in Webland for years—authors might find themselves longing for the traditional review that at least has the virtue of disappearing from public view with yesterday's news.

The traditional review is the only kind of "coverage" that focuses exclusively on the text and that is—or at least aims to be—written by a disinterested and qualified critic. For authors, favorable reviews from such critics can emotionally offset poor sales, and sometimes can do so practically: for the publisher on the verge of dropping a poorly selling author, good reviews from respectable critics have in the past, and should, make a difference. And negative reviews can be useful, even for authors. Authors are fond of saying that they have nothing to learn from their critics, but I suggest that in some cool moment, some years on, they reread their reviews with care. Reviewers don't always get it wrong.

Whatever their value to publishers and authors, reviews are essentially middlemen between books and readers, and the central question is whether books and readers need them or would be served by other kinds of commentary just as well.

Certainly, if the measure is information—titles, availability, news—readers have never been better supplied. Thanks to the Web, the publication of any book, publication data fully included, can be easily posted by publishers or booksellers and easily accessed by readers at minimal cost to either side. The Amazon site itself provides an extraordinary—and expanding—bibliographic record with an excellent search engine that enables readers to find specific titles they're looking for or categories of books they might want to browse. The Web, with its broad distribution, has also enabled review sites and discussion lists (which often carry reader-reviews) to reach groups of readers who share particular interests, and among the great assortment of blogs, some offer sophisticated commentary on books and the book world.

Some of the newer book coverage has generated involvement and enthusiasm, as print reviews, I think, seldom do. Television book clubs, notably Oprah's, but also others to a lesser degree, with their appropriately chosen selections and author appearances, have won enormous numbers of readers for their choices. Online discussions—those with book review editors, for example—allow for instant reader communications: while a letter to the editor of a print publication will not appear for weeks, and needs to be formally (or at least grammatically) written to be published, online questions and responses in these forums not only appear immediately but can be dashed off in the most casual prose. The readers' guides that now accompany many books, which help readers ask questions about what they're reading, seem, by mimicking the analysis of reviewing, to render the reviewer as interpreter unnecessary. And there is no lack of "nontraditional" reviews: thousands of readers on our bookselling Web sites have their say, and their vote, producing a Zagat guide for books which readers can not only use but help create.

But readers frustrated that traditional reviews make an inadequate selection, overlooking significant books, won't find the problem solved by these alternatives. Most book features and media appearances are awarded to books from major presses, which have the clout, money, and personnel to arrange for such publicity, and to books written by well-known names or on topical subjects, which will attract an audience. These are much the same books that receive traditional reviews in the mainstream press. Neither significance nor quality necessarily plays a role in the choice. Book clubs choose books that the selector likes, that have the potential to be enjoyed by a mass audience, and that can be sold in this way, whether or not they are significant. And unlike review editors at publications, editors of personal Web sites and blogs or readers at bookselling

Web sites aren't sent a broad range of thousands of books to select from. These nontraditional reviewers may choose books about which they have something to say, which is all to the good if that something is worthwhile. But the choice, based on the relatively few books they have managed to get hold of and read, is inevitably less comparative than even the inadequate traditional selection and can't inform readers about the relative value of their choices.

Readers dismayed by the lack of criticism in reviews won't find more of it in other coverage, most of which is promotion, sometimes in disguise. Newspaper book features—profiles and interviews—are promotional. Readings are promotional. "Reviews" written by booksellers, even independent booksellers, are promotional. Book clubs are promotional. Even readers' guides are promotional: produced by the publishers to enhance the books' value for—and sales to—reading groups, they may be designed to encourage more thoughtful reading, but they don't encourage a critical approach. None of the guides seem to ask readers to question the quality of a book's prose, its clichéd characterization, or the problems in its story line. They start from the premise that the books are good, and it's their purpose to help readers "understand" why they're good, not discover that they aren't.

Nor will readers frustrated by the quality of criticism in traditional reviewing find it improved in its nontraditional counterparts. On the contrary, in self-published reviews on the Web—the main nontraditional alternative—critical failings are and are bound to be exacerbated. It may be that editors too often fail to do their job in ensuring that reviews are unbiased, informed, well written, or critically astute, but I don't see how it can possibly be an improvement to eliminate the role of editor, the readers' only chance for quality control. Unscreened, anonymous, and unedited, self-published reviewers can be—and often are—as biased, uninformed, ungrammatical, and critically illiterate as they like.

As a replacement for traditional reviewing, the Zagat-style reviewing on Amazon fails above all because it's based on the false premise that all that readers want or need are opinions, any opinions. But random opinions in themselves have little value in helping readers select the books they want to read: the personal recommendation—thumbs up, thumbs down—is useful only if we know the thumbprint, the taste of the person making the recommendation, which determines whether we're likely to agree or disagree. And opinions are only of value in determining what's worthwhile if the taste and judgment are themselves worthwhile; taste may vary, but there is nonetheless good taste and bad, educated judgment and that which is poorly informed. Literary worth has never been a popularity contest, and the majority of the bestsellers of the past have disappeared, some exceptions (i.e., Dickens's novels) notwithstanding. The book on Amazon with 600 high ratings may indeed be good. But to be useful to readers, these unknown reader-reviewers, like professional reviewers, have to make their case, which is what the well-written, well-argued review does. Reader-reviewers can do this: there's nothing to stop a reader from posting a well-conceived review, and many do. But a system that exercises no control over reviews doesn't encourage it. In view of the evident difficulty of writing good reviews, on what basis can we expect to find a multitude of them on Amazon? And does anyone really want to read through six hundred reviews of a single book, each with its own description and evaluation, to try to identify the good ones? I can think of few reading experiences less rewarding; the scrolling alone would be wearing, and by the time I'd read a few dozen reviews, I suspect I'd no longer either need or want to read the book.

In some sense, no commentary can serve readers well unless it also serves books—both individually, by giving each its chance and its due, and collectively, by discerning and promoting quality. No doubt if books could talk, they would complain—with publishers, authors, and readers—that reviews don't serve them very well at all. They would argue that reviewing puts them at the mercy of editors who can ignore them or assign them to biased or ignorant reviewers who are free to treat them shabbily, misrepresent them, trash them without understanding them or praise them for all the wrong reasons. They would say that reviewers so fail to really engage with them that their reviews, dull and lifeless, fail to engage readers. Many forgotten books would claim that had reviewers brought them to life, they might be alive today.

The complaints would be justified. And yet I don't see how books would fare better in the hands of reader-reviewers who—with even fewer checks on bias and conflicting interests, ignorance and accuracy—are still more likely to subject them to the drubbing of their enemies and the meaningless praise of their friends. I don't see how books would fare better in coverage where they're forced to play second fiddle to authors, who ignore them to discuss their early childhood or their marriage, their writing habits and favorite foods, or describe what they aimed for in their work, which often bears little resemblance to what they actually wrote. And once quality is irrelevant in commentary, it becomes irrelevant in books as well: only bad books have something to gain.

Reviews, because they focus on actual texts, can discuss books without the hoopla of publicity or the sideshow of personality, can describe them dispassionately, and can help make difficult work accessible. Because reviews can be critical, they can distinguish and help define quality. On a book page, it is the books that matter, and so reviews chronicle the influence books have on the cultural trends and ideas of a particular time. And if, like all literary commentary, reviews belong to a particular time, nonetheless, as the reference librarian Phyllis Holman Weisbard points out in her essay "Reviews and Their Afterlife,"[13] reviews do have an afterlife. However ephemeral, reviews remain a resource for researchers seeking evaluations of the work of past authors, for publishers seeking books worth reprinting, for insight into another era. While a writer's collection of old reviews often serves mainly to expose the limitations of the genre, providing a context in which even the good critiques seem dated and, if the books under discussion have been forgotten, seem to hang on nothing, the various series that gather contemporary reviews of authors whose work has lasted (the Critical Heritage series, for example) have proven to be interesting and useful. How the work of Chekhov, Melville, Woolf, Hemingway, James, or Wharton was received tells us more than simply whether reviewers got it "right" in admiring them or "wrong" in panning them (the "Rotten Reviews" approach to literary journalism), however entertaining that can be. What reviewers chose to say and what they didn't say, what issues they raised or ignored, opens up a view of other cultural times and a perspective on our own. I can't imagine our alternative coverage leaving a comparable record. So many of our book "features" are commercially oriented and devoid of content, so many of our reader-reviews manipulated and devoid of content, they hardly seem worth saving.

Books—like publishers, authors, and readers—need commentary that is impartial, informed, and critical, and reviewing, however badly it has performed, is by design, by intention, and by the ethics of the field, more disinterested, informed, and critical than the alternative coverage we have today. We need better, not fewer, reviews, and not surrogates that are in the most essential ways not substitutes at all.

Improving the Trade

> Reviewing, like other fallen activities, is never quite perfect; looking on the bright side, however, this means there is always room for improvement.
>
> —NB, *Times Literary Supplement*, December 29, 1995

*I*n reviewing American reviewing, not even the most seasoned of hacks would claim that its "flaws" are "minor." The question is what realistically can be done to improve a trade so unruly, so dependent on individuals, and so constrained by obstacles that lie outside its control. It's very tempting, I think, to be unrealistic about the field, to approach it with reformist zeal, imagining extraordinary criticism that could never be sustained within the genre achieved by simplistic means— longer or shorter reviews, a more popular or literary focus, a call for less praise. But good reviewing will only emerge in a system that fosters it by skillfully negotiating what seem to me the principal obstacles that daunt the field: the oversupply of books, the undersupply of funds, and the absence of critical education among reviewers and readers alike.

First, and most essentially, I think, we need to devise better means of choosing books for review. Our current system inevitably leads to over-looking good books, overpraising bad ones, and undermining the book page. Obviously, from the perspective of reviewing, there are simply too many books. It may be that publishing, for the health of the industry, should reduce its total production, but it's hard to see how competing publishers could ever band together to bring this about. Nor would it necessarily be a good thing if they did. The most likely candidates for deletion would probably be the least profitable books—so much for lit-erary fiction, poetry, serious nonfiction on unfashionable topics, the kinds of books which often have cultural impact, which may actually last, and which sometimes prove, in the long run, to be the most profitable books of all. In any case, nowadays, if publishers did drastically cut their lists, writers could easily publish their own work, and undoubtedly would: self-publishing is easy, inexpensive, and on the rise. If self-published books came to include many of the better midlist works cut by publishers, review editors could no longer afford to ignore them, as they now for the most part do. Selection would be more difficult than ever.

Just how extreme the problem has become is evident in a radical solution that has appeared in recent years: reviews for hire. In 2001, overwhelmed by the increasing number of reviewable books they were forced to reject, the editors of *ForeWord* magazine, a trade publication that focuses on reviewing books from independent presses, decided to start a second, online only, service in which any publisher or author could have their work reviewed—for a fee. In 2004, *Kirkus,* in an effort to bring attention to "overlooked" titles, launched Kirkus Discoveries, which reviews any book, "whether conventionally published, self-published, e-published, published via Print-On-Demand, or not previously published at all"—for a fee. And, in a similar vein, one of the newly developed online review publications, BookReview.com, facing "an avalanche of new books," began offering listings-for-pay as well as an "Express Review Service"—which takes books to "the top of the reviewers' pile"—at a higher price.[1]

Not too surprisingly, pay-per-review schemes have generated controversy in the reviewing community, with some critics expressing a mix of outrage and scorn: reviews that have been "bought" raise obvious questions about ethics and credibility. Who, critics say, would trust such reviews? Publications that offer them don't promise their clients favorable assessments, and you could argue, as *ForeWord* did,[2] that a fee doesn't necessarily predetermine a favorable review; theoretically, at least, the two can be separate. You could also argue that pay-per-review isn't so very different from the traditional approach, that publishers have always paid for reviews, if indirectly, by paying for advertising space, which is one reason, after all, that books published by the commercial presses, which advertise, have been more frequently reviewed than books from the small and university presses, which seldom advertise and are largely ignored.

What we've traditionally had, though, is unsatisfactory, and a pay-per-review scheme, with its inbuilt conflict of interest, is all too likely to make it worse. Disinterest is hard enough to achieve in reviewing without challenging it still further. But what is most centrally wrong with the selling of reviews, it seems to me, is the fact that it divests reviewing of one of its central functions: meaningful selection. As readers, we count on reviewing to discuss the books that matter, to recommend which books to read. The value of being told that four insignificant books are indeed insignificant is small if five excellent ones were ignored because their publishers couldn't afford a review. Unless the books reviewed are the ones we want and need to know about, why read reviews at all? If our selection methods are inadequate, we need to find better methods, not do away with purposeful selection altogether.

Second, we need to find better ways to reward reviewers. Dismal fees make it hard for competent reviewers to do an adequate job, and they may encourage them to abandon reviewing, leaving the field to the less competent or to writers who review for the wrong reasons—as an easy way to get into print, to promote a particular viewpoint, or to publicize their own books. Poor pay, which has always been a factor in poor reviewing, may be still more significant today, when it's neither desirable nor even possible to live the marginal literary life many people aspired to in earlier decades, when poverty in a literary cause had a cachet it no longer enjoys.

But the most recent survey of pay rates for reviewers shows that fees are as dismal as ever. Nor do prospects for the future look good. It's doubtful that publishers concerned that book pages aren't profitable are going to consider making them still less profitable by raising reviewers' wages, or that review editors who are now seeking to make their book pages more economically viable through such nonreviewing efforts as book clubs and book fairs will be able to provide additional funds, should they find them, to reviewers. The volunteer reviewers on Amazon and other book Web sites have probably not helped the cause of higher pay among periodical publishers who care little about the book page, reinforcing as they do the sense that reviewing is something people want to do—i.e., that it's fun, not work—and that it's something anyone can do, since it's now something everyone does, rather than skilled work deserving of compensation.

Third, we need to better train—or as Stuart P. Sherman said, "develop"[3]—reviewers and review editors, better preparing them for the technical constraints and demands of the genre and, more broadly, alerting them to critical and ethical issues in the field. Critical talent, like all talent, may be rare, but if superb reviewers will always be in short supply, we can increase the number of good ones if we can find ways to educate critics.

In part this involves helping reviewers cope with American ambivalence toward criticism, the trait characterized by Henry James as "our native mistrust for intellectual discretion." On the one hand, criticism has been equated with elitism, and on the other, with nastiness. Unfortunately, our more intellectual publications have tended to confirm both of these images, ignoring by and large books likely to be widely read, and too often replacing the fervor of enthusiasm with the fervor of antagonism, turning reviews into what the critic Wayne Koestenbaum has called "the exercise of sanctioned aggression."[4] Such criticism is no more a solution to building support for good reviewing than it is for providing it. But by contrast, reviews in the general press have tended to ward off charges of elitism and nastiness by dumbing down the tone of reviews to make them accessible and downplaying negative criticism altogether. This effort has resulted in reviews so gutted of interest that they have not only failed to attract the readers they seem designed to woo, they've disappointed the readers they had. There is a mode between these extremes that more reviewers need to find.

As a means of educating reviewers, the courses in reviewing that have begun to emerge in recent years in various media programs seem to me as yet of limited value. On the upside, their existence implies to potential reviewers that there is something to learn, that reviewing involves more than simply reading a book and saying what one thinks. They can introduce and explore ethical issues too often ignored in the field, and to the degree that they teach basic reading and writing, skills neglected in our schools, they're obviously useful. As a side effect, teaching these courses can provide an additional source of income for impoverished reviewers. And though I find it doubtful that stretching overstretched reviewers still further by burdening them with yet another poverty-wage job—teaching adjunct (no benefits)—is better than rewarding them for improving their reviews, as a longtime writing teacher, I believe that teaching writing can make teachers themselves more aware as writers, or, in this case, as reviewers.

But teachers will be facing students who have already learned about reviewing by reading many poor reviews, and who have assumed that they were good because they were published. Even the best of reviewer-teachers will have trouble discouraging these students, who are eager to get published, from imitating these bad reviews so long as they see them as publishable. And of course if the teachers themselves are reviewers currently participating in a system of mediocre reviewing, and perhaps themselves writing mediocre reviews, they'll merely pass along bad habits, perpetuating what we have. Though it may sound circular to say it, I doubt such courses can be effective unless the standards of reviewing are already raised within the field.

So far, the most promising effort to inform reviewers and editors and help them grapple with the difficulties of the field has been the National Book Critics Circle, founded in 1974 "to encourage and raise the quality of book criticism in all media, and to provide for an exchange of information between fellow professionals." Comprising both reviewers and review editors, this group has addressed intellectual, practical, and ethical aspects of reviewing in its newsletters, in its surveys, and in panel discussions at annual membership meetings. As a member for more than ten years, I've appreciated the organization's efforts to raise awareness both in and out of the field and to provide a sense of community: working in isolation, it's easy to feel that you're writing in and into a void.

But despite its promise, the effectiveness of the National Book Critics Circle has been limited. Its New York location has made annual meetings inaccessible for the many reviewers across the country who can scarcely afford to travel to Manhattan on wages that barely cover transportation to the library. Lack of funds has kept the organization dependent on volunteer labor, which is especially difficult to sustain with a workforce whose paid work veers dangerously close to volunteer labor. And despite its aim of benefiting all of its members, past newsletters reveal a split that I have certainly felt between the elected twenty-four-person board and the general members. Board members get both symbolic and actual perks: their names are on the NBCC stationery; they determine the NBCC's annual literary awards, which gives them a chance to meet and discuss books; they present the awards, which gives them a chance to mingle with the award-winners as well as the New York publishing community—all of which enhances the opportunities for reviewing contacts and assignments. By contrast, general members get mainly a newsletter for their dues. It seems to me that there are serious problems with this two-tier system, which saps the organization of energy, both by fostering a sense of inequality and by making it hard for anyone but board members to participate, though the recent shift to online communications—for newsletters, e-mail communications, and a blog—may help make the organization more open.

Most disappointingly, in recent years, the National Book Critics Circle has devoted most of its energies and resources to the annual awarding of literary prizes and a reviewing citation. Whether the citation, awarded to a single reviewer, can be said even theoretically to help raise the level of reviewing is at best debatable. I find it difficult to believe that many reviewers will work harder on their reviews in the hope of receiving an award they know they have little chance to win, and I wonder whether efforts to win would lead to better or simply more flashy reviews. But surely, in view of the organization's aims, it has been misguided to be so focused on the other literary prizes, which do nothing to improve reviewing, which do little to encourage the exchange of information between any professionals but the twenty-four members of the board who decide upon them, and which, like all awards, it seems to me, represent the worst aspect of reviewing: the hyperbole. The reasoning behind this effort may be that by winning prestige for the prizes the organization can garner prestige for itself and reviewing as well. But I don't see that this has happened; book reviewing remains as lowly and undervalued as ever.

It would be naive to minimize the impact of these obstacles on reviewing or to exaggerate what the reviewing community on its own can do about them. Neither reviewers nor review editors publish books, and they can do nothing to reduce their numbers; they have nothing to sell but their wares, which clearly do not command a high price in the marketplace; they can neither make reviewing easier than it is nor make American culture more intellectual than it is. But that we can only do the doable doesn't mean we can do nothing. If editors and reviewers can't change the culture, they can change the culture of reviewing, which I think could be transformed by even modest shifts in formats, conceptions, and traditions.

If better reviewing is to emerge, it seems to me it will be the editors who make it happen. I realize that this seems counterintuitive: reviewers write the reviews. But editors, however invisible, create the setting in which reviews are written and published. It's the editor who selects the books and assigns them their measure of space. It's the editor who selects reviewers, and by accepting, rejecting, editing, or neglecting to edit their work, determines what will be discussed and even what kinds of things will be said. It's the editor, at work behind the scenes, who in fact holds center stage.

A question I would start with is why our editors as editors are so often invisible. If one of the most basic aims of reviewing is to give readers some coherent sense of the current book world, more editorial commentary would certainly be welcome. Yet where are the editors of our book pages? Few readers know their names, let alone their aims for their book sections. Some editors write columns or reviews. The *New York Times Book Review* now includes "Upfront," a brief note from the anonymous editors about a book reviewed in that issue. But only rarely—at the *Atlantic Monthly,* for example—do editors appear as editors, offering readers insight into what is on the page: why these books, why not others, what is reflected in the choices.

As magazine editors write brief introductions to every issue, the review editor might provide observations that would reveal to readers the philosophy underlying the book page, adding a dimension to the reviews and more fully engaging readers. Unlike most book "features," which shift attention away from criticism, this commentary would focus on the reviews and might help elicit reader correspondence which, with its lively gripes and disagreements, is such a dynamic part of a book page, is so often missing, and needs to be actively encouraged. In the meantime, the very act of describing their philosophy would help editors define it and force them to look more closely at where their book pages, by their own aims and standards, succeed and fail.

Another question I would ask is why, if editors want to give readers a coherent sense of the book world, so many fail to organize their book sections more coherently. I find it extraordinary that while some book sections sensibly group together reviews of books by category—fiction, biography, and so forth—many, including our largest, the *New York Times Book Review,* present reviews with little discernible pattern. Apart from the leading titles in the *New York Times Book Review,* which I assume to be books of special interest, I feel that I'm encountering a hodgepodge series of books, which forces me to jump from topic to topic and genre to genre, prevents me from finding at a glance the kinds of books that interest me, and is intellectually disconcerting: the randomness of the arrangement conveys a sense of a random selection. By grouping books together, editors can help readers grasp what kinds of books are being published, compare different books within a category, and—because the books have been given a context—think more intelligently about the reviews they're reading. A meaningful arrangement conveys the sense that selection has been meaningful, and it may be that selection will become more meaningful as editors, in creating order on the book page, better organize the book world for themselves.

If editors, faced with thousands of books, will inevitably make inappropriate choices, they can obviously ensure a better selection if they can get more of the candidates examined by critics they trust. They could do this if they relied more upon columnists to handle books in specific fields. This is hardly a new idea, but it has been used predominantly for genre books, which have been grouped in roundup columns; while some book pages, such as the book section of the *Boston Sunday Globe,* have expanded their use of columnists, most editors haven't given the practice the broad use I think it deserves. Unlike the editor, a columnist in a particular field can actually read through dozens of books in that field each month, or at least through enough of each to form an opinion on whether it ought to be reviewed. Not every word must be read at this stage—a book is only being assessed for selection, not reviewed. The quality of a book is generally evident in its organization, its prose, its opening chapters, its conclusion. This is obviously more true of nonfiction than it is of fiction, but in most cases, even fiction can be broadly evaluated at this level by an experienced reader. And the columnist in a field becomes experienced. Because he's covering a field, he'll have a more educated sense than the editor can have of which books matter.

Books will still be overlooked, but fewer will be missed, and fewer still will be missed if columnists are rotated. Although we tend to associate bias with the way in which books are discussed, it obviously plays a role in selection as well. In choosing books for review, I was always aware of my personal preferences, and I tried to balance my choices fairly, but of course if I included the kind of books I didn't like, there was a fairly good chance I wouldn't like them. Since every reviewer has his taste, and his choices will reflect it, the fiction reviewer who likes a "good old-fashioned story" should be balanced by the reviewer who appreciates more innovative fiction; the crime fiction columnist who likes only hard-boiled mysteries should be balanced by the reviewer who likes procedurals or "cozies"; the political reviewer who is conservative should be balanced by the liberal. As columnists appearing on a regular basis, they will be familiar to readers, who will know where they're coming from and how to assess their judgments. If newspapers can achieve this kind of balance on their op-ed pages, I see no reason why they can't achieve it on their book pages as well.

From the reviewer's perspective, the position of columnist is preferable to that of reviewer. For one thing, it *is* a position, as the role of freelance reviewer is not. As a columnist affiliated with a publication, I generally found that people were more likely to consider my reviewing "real work" (if still not quite "my own")—indeed, almost a job—which provided me with some much-needed status: not all rewards are monetary. Since a column doesn't necessarily pay more than a review, many columnists will still lack a salary, or even a decent fee—in fact, it's likely that as a columnist, for the work I did, I earned less. But in a real sense the finances were better, because the work and payment were steady; while as a freelancer, I was forced to drum up new assignments to be paid at all, as a columnist I didn't have to waste time drumming and had a regular fee I could count on. Moreover, where the reviewer by tradition sells his single book for a pittance, the columnist receives and can sell many, and the pittances add up, a necessary addition to his income that may seem minute to outsiders, but that on the reviewer pay scale becomes substantial.

For the columnist covering a field, all reading for his reviews becomes part of the research that reviewers need to do and seldom can. The time saved by the editor who doesn't have to find a match can be used to the reviewer's advantage. Reviewers reading extensively in an area will be more attuned to which books in that field are important, will be able, through comparative reading, to understand their context, will have a grasp of the issues that need to be addressed—both by the book and by the review—and will be better able to evaluate them. Crucially, columnists choose their own books: I was almost always more likely to respond to books I had chosen than to those an editor had simply sent. The books might still be mediocre—I could only choose from what was out there— but I knew why I had chosen them. I had reasons for my review.

Reviewers, of course, should always know why books were chosen. But editors, in my experience, often neglect to give reasons. In some cases, it may be that they think the reasons are obvious. They may consider them unimportant, or lack the time to discuss them. And some editors refrain from discussing books to avoid unduly influencing reviews, a worthy concept that turns out to be a poor practice. Too often reviewers, unaware of the context for selection, end up providing no context. Unless a book is splendid—in which case the reason for the review appears to be the book's quality—their review makes little sense to readers who wonder why the book that was panned or received a tepid assessment was reviewed in the first place. This could be resolved by more dialogue between the editor and the reviewer, who should be told why the editor thinks a book matters enough for a review, with the open understanding that he isn't bound to concur. Reviewers should be encouraged to assess the choice for themselves and reject it if they disagree.

If reviewers returned books they thought had little value, our book pages would dramatically improve. But in our current system of reviewing, such returns are neither expected nor encouraged. Reviewers know that returning a book is likely to displease an editor, whose schedule has now been disrupted, and who now needs to find another book and perhaps match it with a new reviewer. Reviewers themselves, busy with other work and inclined like most people to procrastinate, may not have read the book until so close to the deadline it would be unprofessional to return it. And by the time reviewers have read and assessed a book, they will already have put in hours for which, unless they review the book, they won't be remunerated. Ideally, reviewers would be paid a reading fee for assessing books, which would legitimize returns and compensate them for their time as well. But if few publications have the budget for reading fees, editors can let reviewers know they welcome this assessment, allow time in both their own and reviewers' schedules for those books where it's most likely to occur, and at the very least assure reviewers that they won't be penalized for rejecting books they don't think warrant a review.

If a reviewer should be encouraged to help decide whether a book deserves a review, she should also be encouraged to discuss the kind of space it deserves. The reviewer after all is the one who has actually read the book. This kind of assessment is necessary even for books by "major" authors, where the question isn't usually whether their book will be reviewed but what length the review will be. There should be no automatic choices for full-length or lead reviews. Editors may feel that any new book by John Updike or Philip Roth will need to be included, if only because readers will expect it; but they can consider that if the reviewer thinks it isn't very good, a shorter review might suffice. The decision should really depend on the nature of the failure: a long review is worthwhile if the book is bad in a meaningful way, but not if it's simply bad. Space can be flexibly determined, influenced by the judgment of the reviewer.

By involving reviewers in the process of creating the book page—in choosing books and allotting space—editors will get a better selection of books, a more balanced page, and better reviews. Reviewers will be more aware of what they're doing beyond writing about isolated books or simply fulfilling assignments. After telling an editor that he thinks the latest book by Mr. Major Author isn't very good, he'll be less likely to feel his role is to support the author's reputation.

Along with rethinking the way they choose books, editors should reconsider the way they choose reviewers. Whether they're hiring reviewers or columnists, they need to look for writers who are above all critics: writers who in the sample reviews they submit show critical talent; writers who want to review, and can. It's time to abandon the tradition of accepting and even seeking out reviewers because they've published fiction or written books on subjects that have nothing to do with the books at hand—unless they prove themselves to be critics as well. The idea that "authors" bring status to the book page has been disproven by the fact that our book pages, despite this authorial presence everywhere, have little status. The tradition reinforces the notion that any writer can review, that no particular talent is needed, denying the very skill that is at the heart of reviewing. The practice of favoring celebrated authors over real critics by giving them plum assignments—lead positions for "big" books—suggests that it's an honor to have these people on the book page. But the honorees on the book page should be good critics. If editors don't recognize reviewing as work in its own right, it's hard to imagine who will. Editors alone can cultivate critical talent, so widely neglected outside academia. The book page should help reviewers establish their own recognizable names: again, not all rewards are monetary. Such support would help give reviewers more spine, and it would give readers reviews that are actually reviews.

Because review editors, in contrast with reviewers, have something more closely resembling conventional jobs and are salaried, they escape the view that their reviewing isn't work and are better positioned to alter that view. To gain recognition for the field as a field, they might work to strengthen the National Book Critics Circle, an organization I think the field really needs, using their influence to redirect its energies away from award-giving toward more essential issues in criticism. As editors they are in touch with many reviewers—whose own work keeps them more isolated—and they could use the centralized position they enjoy through their publications to encourage reviewers to participate in the National Book Critics Circle. Since editors work with publishers and publication editors as well as with reviewers and see thousands of books and hundreds of reviews, they're bound to have a broader perspective on the field than reviewers, who are focused on writing individual reviews, and could articulate the issues they think the National Book Critics Circle needs to address.

Closer to home, editors need to articulate these issues for their own reviewers by drawing up guidelines that are sent out with every assignment to every columnist and reviewer. Critics have decried the absence of ethical guidelines at most publications, but equally surprising is the general absence of any guidelines at all. Do editors assume that all potential reviewers know precisely what constitutes a good review? The evidence provided by our reviewing suggests this isn't a wise assumption. If editors want something better, they'll have a far greater chance of getting it if they describe what "better" would be. This is the editor's chance to define what he means by good reviewing in general, and what he wants more specifically for his own book page. As in articulating a philosophy for readers, the act of writing in itself would help formulate his aims. As every editor realizes, even if he hasn't read E. M. Forster, he will only know what he thinks when he sees what he has said.

I see these guidelines describing, at a minimum, the basic editorial expectations for a review, the elements which are so fundamental an editor couldn't discuss them with a reviewer without insulting him, but which, put in writing, are simply policies—objective, impersonal, universal, and required: the need for a concise description of the book that gets to the heart of what it's about and is neither an endless plot summary nor an account of its contents; and the need for an evaluation. They could describe the more particular goals of an individual book page, indicating the kinds of books the editor wants to be discussing (books likely to be neglected? or likely to be popular?), which would help reviewers in making their own selection decisions; and they could describe the general way the editor wants these books to be discussed: the language, the tone, the level of expertise.

The guidelines might remind reviewers that they are critics, that it isn't acceptable to write only favorable reviews or to review only books they like, that their job is not to sell, promote, or advertise books, nor to comfort authors for their failures, no matter how many years it took to produce them, but to be critical. They might point out that "critical" is not synonymous with nasty, both to liberate reviewers from this American association and also to discourage venom.

This would be the place to remind reviewers that the concept of fairness applies not only to authors but also to readers, who want honest opinions. It could also be the place to point out that what is wanted is an opinion, not an objective judgment or a grand statement for all time, which might help reviewers steer clear of highfalutin judgments about masterpieces and monuments, and might actually come as a relief, freeing them to say what they actually think about a book in a way that is more interesting, vital, and real. Finally, these guidelines should of course take in ethics, explicitly defining the kinds of relationships that aren't acceptable or allowed: no reviewing books written by friends, or by friends of friends, or by enemies—no personal relationships of any kind, and if in doubt, bow out.

Setting all of this down in two or three pages—and I don't think it would need more—would force editors to clarify policies that are often left vague; mailing them out with every book would not only make reviewers aware of expectations, but would also keep the issues fresh in editors' minds and fortify them for the task that is often left undone: editing. Reviews are edited so poorly they often appear not to have been edited at all. The main problem isn't copyediting, though as in all journalism errors in syntax and grammar certainly occur. The more troubling issue is the apparent absence of editorial control on questions of coherence, persuasiveness, accuracy, meaning, and the fulfillment of basic literary aims.

Why this absence of editorial control? Review editors, I've found, aren't shy. Undoubtedly, most are overworked, underpaid, and generally harried. They're aware that they need to be wary: all changes, even grammatical edits, can alter meaning; they need to be on guard against influencing reviewers' opinions of books they themselves haven't read, written by authors they themselves may like or dislike, on topics about which they may have views of their own. But none of this explains why editors run reviews that are missing the central ingredients of a review (a description and an assessment), that contain sentences devoid of meaning, that give away the entire plot, that are filled with clichés.

Review editors may lack time, but they aren't dealing with breaking news. And they're hardly alone in having to worry about unintentional changes they may inflict: but they shouldn't be inflicting changes. Points can be queried, gaps, excesses, lapses in logic flagged, reviewese returned for revision. When an editor who actually edited caught me calling a first novel "impressive" and asked for a change, she didn't force me to distort what I really thought but helped me to define it—and embarrassed me sufficiently that I never used the cliché again. Querying, flagging, asking for revisions—these are standard editorial procedures, from which no writer should be exempt. All writers need editors, even major authors— perhaps major authors most of all—and even editors who themselves review, who should submit their copy to their own editors. The result would be reviews far more accurate than what we have, far more likely to earn reader trust, and far more pleasurable to read.

Ultimately, of course, the quality of the book page comes down to the reviews, which are in the hands of the reviewers. Editors can't provide insights into books they haven't read, can't supply the taste a reviewer lacks, and can only do so much for humdrum prose. If reviewers don't read carefully, only the authors will know, and if reviewers respond dishonestly, not even the authors will know. Only reviewers can be brave enough to write what they think even if no one else agrees, and astute enough to realize that independent judgment is the only worthwhile judgment.

Ideally, all reviewers would bring their own guidelines to the job, a set of rules more stringent than any editor could apply. Some do. L. E. Sissman set forth a list of proscriptions he devised (and presumably followed) as a critic in his thoughtful essay "Reviewer's Dues."[5] Many reviewers, I suspect, would be as surprised as I was at their scope. Alongside many injunctions we would expect, such as "Never review the work of a friend," "Never review the work of an enemy," "Never climb on bandwagons," and "Never fail to give the reader a judgment and a recommendation on the book. And tell why," Sissman posed less obvious strictures, such as "Never review a book in a field you don't know or care about," "Never read the jacket copy or the publisher's handout before reading and reviewing a book," and "Never fail to take chances in judgment." But our reviews suggest that many reviewers have no such list of "moral imperatives," as Sissman called his strictures, and many will never develop one if they see such rules contradicted daily by reviewers who climb on bandwagons, neglect to give judgments of books (or to tell why), and take no chances whatsoever in their judgments, and yet get published—in prestigious places—all the same. In a field where reviewers who write sophomoric criticism can appear in our leading publications and reviewers who write meaningless sentences can win prizes in criticism, reviewers will have no incentive to do better. In the end, though, for all that we might say that reviewers ought to do this or that, only editors can demand it, encourage it, and finally enforce it, by refusing to run inadequate reviews.

Underlying these less-than-radical suggestions are the premises that underlie my view of the trade, which are also less than radical but not, I think, universally shared: That not only is reviewing important, but reviewers and editors need to take its importance more seriously than they do, steeling themselves against public opinion, literary snobbery, and their own self-doubt and remembering that cultural attitudes are subject to change. That whatever the intrinsic problems in the field, the traditions have an enormous impact on its quality, and new traditions can be established. That not only can reviewing, however insufficient its resources, require standards, competence, and accountability, but by demanding them—and only by demanding them—actually acquire them. And that while this is a trade that takes pride in individuality and often seems not just to accept but to enjoy its characteristic disorder, the reviewing community needs to come together to clarify, if not codify, the aims of the field.

Whether reviewing, even if it improved, would win the support it needs is debatable; so many economic and cultural factors are involved. While our book pages could certainly draw new readers and bring back those who have abandoned them, the audience would not be huge in a country only mildly interested in reading and even less interested in reading reviews, and it might not be large enough for periodicals and advertisers to cater to it. But if it's unreasonable for publishers, authors, and readers to expect superb reviewing that they do little to support, it's still more un-reasonable for reviewers and editors to expect support for a product that fails to do its job.

At a time when the number of books is soaring and interest in literary works falling, when anti-elitists claim that quality is relative and every book is good in its own way, the need is greater than ever for critical guid-ance that will not only help sort the good from the bad but show why the difference matters. Surely it's time to abandon the notion that reviewing is forever doomed to be, in the words of one historian, "no better than it should be,"[6] to revise the tired tale of its perpetual decline, and to provide that critical guidance which is the central work of the trade.

Notes

Introduction: The Reviewer's Lament

1. Bill Marx, "The Decline of Book Reviewing."

2. Andrew Greeley, "Who Reads Book Reviews Anyway?"; John Hollander, "Some Animadversions on Current Reviewing," 224; Max Gissen, "Commercial Criticism and Punch-Drunk Reviewing," 252; Helen E. Haines, "Book Reviewing in Review," 733; Edmund Wilson, "The All-Star Literary Vaudeville," in *The Shores of Light: A Literary Chronicle of the Twenties and Thirties*, 229; *Bookman*, September 1897, 45; *Scribner's Monthly*, March 1875, 626; *Nation*, July 6, 1865, 11; *Mirror*, October 10, 1833, 47; *Portico*, June 1817, 458–59; *Monthly Anthology*, December 1805, 620–22.

3. Joan Shelley Rubin, *The Making of Middlebrow Culture*, 34. Rubin relates "the American affinity for diagnoses of declension—for seeing in the present a waning of earlier glories"—to book reviewing.

4. Frank Luther Mott, *A History of American Magazines*, 1:408.

5. Reviewers' frequent use of unsourced information is readily apparent. But to discern inconsistent descriptions requires reading many reviews of a book. See my essay "Inside Book Reviewing," based, in part, on comparisons of reviews of *A Mother's Work*. "Day Care vs. Being There," review of *A Mother's Work*, by Deborah Fallows, *New York Times Book Review*, October 27, 1985, 12; Review of *A Mother's Work*, by Deborah Fallows, *Radcliffe Quarterly*, June 1986, 48.

6. Review of *Blue Shoe*, by Anne Lamott, *Minneapolis Star Tribune*, October 6, 2002, www.startribune.com.

7. Comment on Ian McEwan in "Literature's Cuckold," review of *Love, Etc.*, by Julian Barnes, *New Republic*, April 2, 2001, 36.

8. "Ghost Story," review of *Anil's Ghost*, by Michael Ondaatje, *Boston Sunday Globe*, April 30, 2000, J1, J4; "Looking for Revelation in All the Wrong Places," review of *The Book of Revelation*, by Rupert Thomson, *Boston Sunday Globe*, April 30, 2000, J2; Short Takes, review of *A Girl with a Monkey*, by Leonard Michaels, *Boston Sunday Globe*, April 30, 2000, J2; "Writing the Novel's Future," review of

White Teeth, by Zadie Smith, *Boston Sunday Globe,* April 30, 2000, J1; "The Dark Descent," review of *The Black Veil: A Memoir with Digressions,* by Rick Moody, *Washington Post Book World,* May 26, 2002, 5; review of *True History of the Kelly Gang,* by Peter Carey, *Boston Book Review,* April 2001, www.bookwire.com/bbr/bbr-home.html; review of *The Autograph Man,* by Zadie Smith, *Salon,* September 5, 2002, www.salon.com.

9. "A.A.R.P. Recruits," review of *Middle Age,* by Joyce Carol Oates, *New York Times Book Review,* September 16, 2001, 7.

10. "Oddities and Ends: Irving Unveils Another Gallery of Grotesques," review of *Until I Find You,* by John Irving, *Boston Sunday Globe,* July 10, 2005, E9.

11. Review of *The Corrections,* by Jonathan Franzen, *New York Times Book Review,* September 9, 2001, 10–12.

12. Martin Amis, *The War against Cliché,* 370; Victoria Glendinning, "The Book Reviewer: The Last Amateur?" 190; Peter S. Prescott, preface to *Never in Doubt: Critical Essays on American Books, 1972–1985* (New York: Arbor House, 1986), 3.

13. Joseph Epstein, "Reviewing and Being Reviewed," 51.

14. W. H. Auden, "A Disturbing Novelist: On Muriel Spark's *A Muriel Spark Trio,"* in *A Company of Readers: Uncollected Writings of W. H. Auden, Jacques Barzun, and Lionel Trilling from the Readers' Subscription and Mid-Century Book Clubs,* ed. Arthur Krystal, 150.

15. Virginia Woolf, *Reviewing,* 7.

16. H. L. Mencken, "Criticism of Criticism of Criticism," 189.

17. John Simon, introduction to *The Sheep from the Goats: Selected Literary Essays of John Simon* (New York: Weidenfeld and Nicolson, 1989), xix.

18. Anthony Brandt, introduction to *Rotten Reviews: A Literary Companion,* 12.

19. Introduction to "Reporting the Arts II," National Arts Journalism Program, 10.

20. Ibid., 13.

21. Ibid.

22. Bill Marx, "Critical Condition," 79; John Simon, "Everybody's a Critic," review of *Regarding Film: Criticism and Comment,* by Stanley Kauffmann; *Citizen Sarris: American Film Critic,* ed. Emanuel Levy, *Los Angeles Times,* March 24, 2002, www.latimes.com.

Unnatural Selection

1. Motion Picture Association of America, Research and Statistics: Frequently Asked Questions, www.mpaa.org.

2. Florin L. McDonald, "Book Reviewing in the American Newspaper," 15.

3. Pat Holt, Holt Uncensored #361, March 7, 2003, www.holtuncensored.com.

4. Nora Rawlinson, "A Change in the 'Forecasts.'"

5. Jim Hoberman, "The Film Critic of Tomorrow, Today," in *The Crisis of Criticism,* ed. Maurice Berger, 73.

6. Donald Davidson, "Criticism outside New York," 249–50.

Vermin, Dogs, and Woodpeckers

1. Personal communication to Thomas Christensen.

2. Henry Wadsworth Longfellow, in *Life of Henry Wadsworth Longfellow with Extracts from His Journals and Correspondence,* ed. Samuel Longfellow, 3 vols. (Boston: Houghton Mifflin and Company, 1891), 3:403.

3. Samuel T. Coleridge, "The First Lecture," in *Seven Lectures on Shakespeare and Milton* (London: Chapman and Hall, 1856), 4–5.

4. Greeley, "Who Reads Book Reviews Anyway?"

5. Catharine O'Neill, in *Books, Books, Books: A Hilarious Collection of Literary Cartoons,* ed. S. Gross and Jim Charlton (New York: Harper and Row, 1988).

6. National Book Critics Circle survey.

7. Davidson, "Criticism outside New York," 248.

8. Edward Hower, "Reviewing Books," 24.

9. Norman Podhoretz, "Book Reviewing and Everyone I Know," 259.

10. Edmund Wilson, "The Literary Worker's Polonius," in *The Shores of Light: A Literary Chronicle of the Twenties and Thirties,* 601.

11. Brandon Massey, "Secret #10: Write Book Reviews," www.brandonmassey .com

12. Stuart P. Sherman, letter to Ellery Sedgwick, cited in *The Making of Middlebrow Culture,* by Joan Shelley Rubin, 59.

13. Davidson, "Criticism outside New York," 247.

14. Alan Ross, "Successful Failures," review of *Clever Hearts,* by Hugh and Mirabel Cecil, *Times Literary Supplement,* July 20–26, 1990, 770.

15. Dwight Garner, "Crisis in Critville: Why You Can't Trust Book Reviews."

16. Cyril Connolly, "Ninety Years of Novel Reviewing," in *The Selected Essays of Cyril Connolly,* ed. Peter Quennell, 215.

17. Michael Dorris, "Say, Who Was That Semi-Masked Book Reviewer?"

18. Charles Miner Thompson, "Honest Literary Criticism," 183.

19. Review of *Angela's Ashes,* by Frank McCourt, *Boston Sunday Globe,* August 25, 1996, N13.

The Match

1. Maureen Dowd, "Banks for the Memories," *New York Times,* March 15, 1997, Op-Ed page; "See the Girl with the Red Dress On," review of *Are Men Necessary: When Sexes Collide,* by Maureen Dowd, *New York Times Book Review,* November 13, 2005, 49; Robert Gottlieb, "A Book Editor in Palmy Days; His Stable of Fabulous Beasts," review of *Another Life: A Memoir of Other People,* by Michael Korda, *New York Observer,* April 26, 1999, 28; "Turn, Turn, Turn," review of *Blinded by the Right,* by David Brock, *Washington Post Book World,* March 17, 2002, 6; "Conspiracy Theories," review of *The Hunting of the President,* by Joe Conason and Gene Lyons, *New York Times Book Review,* April 9, 2000, 24.

2. "Restoration Murder," review of *An Instance of the Fingerpost,* by Iain Pears, *New York Times Book Review,* March 22, 1998, 12.

3. Paul Baumann, "Confessions of a Book Review Editor," 84.

4. Henry Holt, *Garrulities of an Octogenarian Editor* (Boston and New York: Houghton Mifflin Company, 1923), 283–84.

5. Baumann, "Confessions of a Book Review Editor," 85.

6. Stanley B. Winters, My Say.

7. George Orwell, "Confessions of a Book Reviewer," in *The Collected Essays, Journalism and Letters of George Orwell,* ed. Sonia Orwell and Ian Angus, 4:183.

8. George Orwell, "In Defence of the Novel," in *The Collected Essays, Journalism and Letters of George Orwell,* ed. Sonia Orwell and Ian Angus, 1:251–52.

9. David Shaw, "Power, Fear of N. Y. Times Book Review," December 12, 1985.

10. Darts and Laurels, *Columbia Journalism Review,* November/December 1991, 38; Anthony Burgess, "Joseph Kell, V. S. Naipaul and Me," 14; "Book Reviewing Ain't Beanbag," Darts and Laurels, *Columbia Journalism Review,* July/August 2000, 14; Robert Gottlieb, "Ms. Adler, *The New Yorker* and Me," article on *Gone: The Last Days of "The New Yorker,"* by Renata Adler, *New York Observer,* January 17, 2000, 13.

11. Norman Mailer, "A Critic with Balance: A Letter from Norman Mailer."

12. Nina King, *National Book Critics Circle Journal,* January 21, 1988, 1.

13. *National Book Critics Circle Journal,* January 21, 1988.

14. Glendinning, "The Book Reviewer: The Last Amateur?" 184.

15. David Shaw, "Papers' Stepchild: Reviewing Books: It's Haphazard," December 11, 1985.

16. Steve Weinberg, "Assigning Book Reviews: A System in Need of Repair?" 2.

17. Larry Swindell, "The Function of a Book Editor," in *Book Reviewing,* ed. Sylvia E. Kamerman, 73–74.

18. Shaw, "Papers' Stepchild."

Getting It Right

1. Gerald Eskenazi, "Unsportsmanlike Conduct?" review of *Interference: How Organized Crime Influences Professional Football*, by Dan E. Moldea, *New York Times Book Review*, September 3, 1989, 8.

2. Edwin Diamond, "Can You *Prove* the Hollandaise Was Curdled?" 34.

3. Eskenazi, "Unsportsmanlike Conduct?"

4. Diamond, "Can You *Prove* the Hollandaise Was Curdled?" 34.

5. Review of *Leaves of Grass*, by Walt Whitman, Frank Leslie's *Illustrated Newspaper*, December 20, 1856, 42; review of *Leaves of Grass*, by Walt Whitman, *Saturday Review*, March 15, 1856, 393–94; Rufus W. Griswold, review of *Leaves of Grass*, by Walt Whitman, *Criterion*, November 10, 1855, 24; Randall Jarrell, *Randall Jarrell's Letters: An Autobiographical and Literary Selection*, ed. Mary Jarrell (Boston: Houghton Mifflin Company, 1985), 44; "The Extremities of Nicholson Baker," review of *Checkpoint*, by Nicholson Baker, *New York Times Book Review*, August 8, 2004, 12–13; "A Little Learning Is a Dangerous Thing," review of *The Know-It-All: One Man's Humble Quest to Become the Smartest Person in the World*, by A. J. Jacobs, *New York Times Book Review*, October 3, 2004, 13; Dale Peck, "The Devil You Know," review of *The Devil's Larder*, by Jim Crace, in *Hatchet Jobs*, 134.

6. Ethel R. Outland, *The "Effingham" Libels on Cooper: A Documentary History of the Libel Suits of James Fenimore Cooper Centering around the Three Mile Point Controversy and the Novel* Home as Found *1837–1845*.

7. Ibid., 78–79.

8. Ibid., 78.

9. Ibid., 92–93, 199.

10. Diamond, "Can You *Prove* the Hollandaise Was Curdled?" 32.

11. Dale Peck, "The Moody Blues," review of *The Black Veil: A Memoir with Digressions*, by Rick Moody, *New Republic*, July 1, 2002, 33; reprinted in *Hatchet Jobs*, 171.

12. Jack Green, *Fire the Bastards!* 15; review of *Vindication*, by Frances Sherwood, *Library Journal*, March 15, 1993, 109; "Her Lips Were Sealed," review of *The Woman Who Wouldn't Talk*, by Susan McDougal, *New York Times Book Review*, January 26, 2003, 14; Corrections, *New York Times*, February 2, 2003.

13. "Updike Has New Story Collection, Angstrom Novella," review of *Licks of Love: Short Stories and a Sequel, "Rabbit Remembered,"* by John Updike, *Houston Chronicle*, August 22, 2001, 14.

14. James Wood, "Human, All Too Inhuman," review of *White Teeth*, by Zadie Smith, *New Republic*, July 24, 2000, 41–45; Daniel Mendelsohn, "Nailed!" review of *Hatchet Jobs: Writings on Contemporary Fiction*, by Dale Peck, *New York Review of Books*, July 15, 2004; Michael Dirda, review of *The Case of the Persevering Maltese: Collected Essays*, by Harry Mathews, and *The Human Country: New and Col-*

lected Stories, by Harry Mathews, *Washington Post Book World,* March 23, 2003, 15.

15. "25 Years Later," review of *Silver Wedding,* by Maeve Binchy, *New York Times Book Review,* September 10, 1989, 18.

16. "Memorable Tales about Everyday Life, Ordinary People," review of *The Whore's Child,* by Richard Russo, *Los Angeles Times,* July 15, 2002.

17. "Coming of Age on Long Island," review of *Child of My Heart,* by Alice McDermott, *Atlantic Monthly,* December 3, 2002, 153.

18. Jacques Barzun, "A Little Matter of Sense," 28.

19. "Dark Family Secrets Cascade from 'The Falls,'" review of *The Falls,* by Joyce Carol Oates, *San Antonio Express-News,* October 17, 2004.

20. "Beating Horror by Becoming Wise," review of *Children and Fools,* by Erich Fried, *New York Times,* January 11, 1995, C18.

21. "At War with Himself," review of *The Complete Works of Isaac Babel, New York Times Book Review,* November 18, 2001, 10–11.

22. "The Electric Psychologist," review of *The Dream Machine: J. C. R. Licklider and the Revolution That Made Computing Personal,* by M. Mitchell Waldrop, *New York Times Book Review,* October 7, 2001, 17.

23. Tom Payne, "Circle of Clichés," *UK Telegraph,* August 8, 2004.

24. Clarkson N. Potter, *Who Does What and Why in Book Publishing,* 101.

25. Ibid., 104.

26. Jack Miles, "Sticks and Stones: Can a Review Be Libelous?" *National Book Critics Circle Journal,* August 1994, 4.

27. David Ansen, "Second Thoughts," *Newsweek,* August 29, 2002, Web exclusive; Harold Clurman, "A Critic's Credo," *Nation,* September 14, 1964, 122.

28. "Leaves of Grass—An Extraordinary Book," review of *Leaves of Grass,* by Walt Whitman, *Brooklyn Daily Eagle,* September 15, 1855, 2.

29. Review of *The Human Country: New and Collected Stories,* by Harry Mathews, *New York Times Book Review,* Books in Brief, October 13, 2002, 28; Dirda, review of *The Case of the Persevering Maltese: Collected Essays,* by Harry Mathews, and *The Human Country: New and Collected Stories,* by Harry Mathews, *Washington Post Book World,* March 23, 2003, 15.

30. Carol Shields, "Wafts of the South," review of *A Writer's Eye: Collected Book Reviews,* by Eudora Welty, *Times Literary Supplement,* August 12, 1994, 20.

31. W. H. Auden, "Two Ways of Poetry: On Philip Larkin's *The Less Deceived* and Geoffrey Hill's *For the Unfallen,*" in *A Company of Readers,* ed. Arthur Krystal, 242.

32. Letters, *Women's Review of Books,* February 1994, 4.

33. Orwell, "Confessions of a Book Reviewer," 4:182.

Private Opinions, Public Forums

1. Garner, "Crisis in Critville."

2. Donald Sheehan, *This Was Publishing: A Chronicle of the Book Trade in the Gilded Age*, 37.

3. "Those Allegations Most Vile," review of *Byron: Life and Legend*, by Fiona MacCarthy, *Times Literary Supplement*, November 8, 2002, 6.

4. "A Troublemaker Walked in Beauty," review of *Byron: Life and Legend*, by Fiona MacCarthy, *New York Times*, December 30, 2002, B12.

5. Harold Clurman, "A Critic's Credo," *Nation*, September 14, 1964, 122.

6. John Tebbel, *The Compact History of the American Newspaper* (New York: Hawthorn Books, Inc., 1969); Chalmers M. Roberts, *The Washington Post: The First 100 Years* (Boston: Houghton Mifflin Company, 1977).

7. John Gross, "'The Littery Supplement' Comes of Age: A History, of Sorts, of the Book Review," 10.

8. Christopher Lehmann-Haupt, "The Daily Newspaper Book Review," in *Book Reviewing*, ed. Sylvia E. Kamerman, 11.

9. Charlotte Austin, "The Art of Reviewing: Book Reviewing Today," The Charlotte Austin Review Ltd.

10. Harriet Klausner, "Amusing Manhattan Romp," review of *The Frog King*, by Adam Davies, October 25, 2002, www.amazon.com.

11. George A. Woods, "Reviewing Books for Children," in *Book Reviewing*, ed. Sylvia E. Kamerman, 63.

12. Orwell, "In Defence of the Novel," 1:252.

13. Thomas Fleming, "The War between Writers and Reviewers," 3.

14. John Maxwell Hamilton, "Inglorious Employment," in *Casanova Was a Book Lover and Other Naked Truths and Provocative Curiosities about the Writing, Selling, and Reading of Books*, 138.

15. Garner, "Crisis in Critville."

Are Book Reviews Necessary?

1. Pat Holt, "Those Dying Book Reviews"; Kevin Berger, "The Incredible Vanishing Book Review"; Craig Lambert, "High Type Culture," *Harvard Magazine*, November–December 1997, 41; Carl Lennertz, "Forrester Says 'Guides' Will Rule," Publishers Lunch, December 20, 2001, www.publishersmarketplace.com.

2. George Stevens and Stanley Unwin, "The Advertising of Books," in *Best-Sellers: Are They Born or Made?* 17.

3. Ibid., 23.

4. Walter Hines Page, *A Publisher's Confession* (Garden City, New York: Dou-

bleday, Page and Company, 1923), 35; J. C. Derby, *Fifty Years among Authors, Books and Publishers* (New York, G. W. Carleton and Company, Publishers, 1884), 240; Sheehan, *This Was Publishing,* 181.

5. Marie Arana-Ward, "Views from Publisher's Row," June 1, 1997.

6. Sarah Lyall, Book Notes, *New York Times,* March 23, 1994, C19.

7. Jim Milliot, "Booksellers Support Selling Efforts, but Could Do Better"; Charlotte Abbott, "The Power of Print Media."

8. Robert Sterling Yard, *The Publisher* (Boston and New York: Houghton Mifflin Company, 1913), 84; Robert Weil, "Making Books: An Executive Editor Speaks His Mind about Publishing Quality Books in a Mass Market Climate," *Washington Post Book World,* February 8, 2004, 8.

9. Michael Joseph, *The Adventure of Publishing* (London: Allan Wingate, 1949), 156–57.

10. Michael Norman, "Reader by Reader and Town by Town, A New Novelist Builds a Following," 28; Arana-Ward, "Views from Publisher's Row"; "Bottom-Line Pressures in Publishing: Is the Critic More Important than Ever?" National Arts Journalism Program, panel discussion, 10; Abbott, "The Power of Print Media," 40.

11. "Outlook 2003: The Hunt for New Readers," *Publishers Weekly,* January 6, 2003, 24.

12. Katha Pollitt, "Thank You for Hating My Book"; Paul Fussell, "Vanity in Review."

13. Phyllis Holman Weisbard, "Reviews and Their Afterlife," 16.

Improving the Trade

1. *ForeWord Magazine,* press release, May 7, 2001. Description of service at www .forewordmagazine.com/clarion; description of services at www.kirkusreviews .com; description of services at www.BookReview.com.

2. *ForeWord Magazine,* press release, May 7, 2001.

3. Rubin, *Making of Middlebrow Culture,* 59.

4. Henry James, "The Madonna of the Future," in *Henry James: Complete Stories, 1864–1874* (New York: Library of America, 1999), 742; Wayne Koestenbaum, "Why Bully Literature?" in *The Crisis of Criticism,* ed. Maurice Berger, 93.

5. L. E. Sissman, "Reviewer's Dues," in *Book Reviewing,* ed. Sylvia Kamerman, 119–125.

6. Mott, *History of American Magazines,* 3:233.

Bibliography

Abbott, Charlotte. "The Power of Print Media." *Publishers Weekly,* May 13, 2002, 39–41.

Almond, Steve. "On Reviews: A First-Timer Reveals How It Feels." *Poets and Writers,* May/June 2003, 44–53.

"Amateurs on Amazon." *Economist.* August 28, 1999, 65.

Amis, Martin. *The War against Cliché: Essays and Reviews, 1971–2000.* New York: Talk Miramax Books/Hyperion, 2001.

Ansen, David. "Second Thoughts." *Newsweek,* August 29, 2002. Web exclusive.

Arana, Marie. Ask the Post. *Washington Post Book World* online, May 11, 2005, transcript, www.washingtonpost.com.

———. Ask the Post. *Washington Post Book World* online, March 29, 2006, transcript, www.washingtonpost.com.

Arana-Ward, Marie. "Views from Publisher's Row." *Washington Post Book World,* June 1, 1997.

Arnold, Martin. "A Critique of the Critics." Making Books. *New York Times,* April 23, 1998, B3.

Avant, John Alfred. "Slouching toward Criticism." *Library Journal,* December 15, 1971, 4055–59.

Bagnall, Nicholas. "O My Connolly and My Toynbee Long Ago!" *New Statesman,* July 4, 1997, 49.

Balakian, Nona. "The Lowly State of Book Reviewing." In *Critical Encounters: Literary Views and Reviews, 1953–1977.* Indianapolis: Bobbs-Merrill, 1978.

Barbato, Joseph. "The Trouble with Reviews." *Publishers Weekly,* April 14, 1989, 28–29.

Barrett, Paul M. "Court Reverses Ruling in Times Case." *Boston Globe,* May 4, 1994, 49.

Barringer, Felicity. "Newspaper Budget Cuts Pinch Book Pages." *New York Times,* April 23, 2001, C8.

Barzun, Jacques. "A Little Matter of Sense." *New York Times Book Review,* June 21, 1987, 1, 27–29.

Bass, Judy. "In Defense of Book Critics." My Say. *Publishers Weekly,* May 8, 1987, 48.

Baumann, Paul. "Confessions of a Book Review Editor." *Columbia Journalism Review,* May/June 2001, 83–85.

Bawer, Bruce. "Literary Life in the 1990s." *New Criterion,* September 1991, 53–60.

Berger, Kevin. "The Incredible Vanishing Book Review." *Salon,* July 19, 2001, www.salon.com.

Berger, Maurice, ed. *The Crisis of Criticism.* New York: New Press, 1998.

Berger, Meyer. *The Story of the New York Times, 1851–1951.* New York: Simon and Schuster, 1951.

Bingham, Sallie. My Say. *Publishers Weekly,* August 5, 1983, 102.

Birkerts, Sven. "Critical Condition: Reading, Writing and Reviewing: An Old-Schooler Looks Back." *BookForum,* Spring 2004, 8–12.

Block, Marylaine. "The Art of Reviewing." *Littera Scripta,* 2000, www.literascripta.com/bibliomania/reviewing.shtml.

Bogart, Leo. "The Culture Beat: A Look at the Numbers." *Gannett Center Journal* (now *Media Studies Journal*), Winter 1990, 23–35.

Bowman, James. "A Little Help for Their Friends." *National Review,* March 7, 1994, 63–67.

———. "Oh Yeah? Says Who? No More Anonymous Reviews, Please." OpinionJournal, *Wall Street Journal,* editorial page, January 14, 2005, www.opinionjournal.com.

Brockes, Emma. "Trash Your Rivals and Get Away with It." *Guardian Unlimited,* January 20, 2000, www.guardian.co.uk.

Bryant, Eric. "Are Reviewers Fair to Gay and Lesbian Writers?" *National Book Critics Circle Journal,* Autumn 1999, 4–5.

Burgess, Anthony. "Joseph Kell, V. S. Naipaul and Me." *New York Times Book Review,* April 21, 1991, 1, 28–31.

Calame, Byron. "The Book Review: Who Critiques Whom—and Why?"

New York Times, December 18, 2005, the Public Editor, Week in Review, 12.

Caldwell, Heather. "Pecked." *Salon,* July 24, 2002, www.salon.com.

Canby, Henry Seidel. *Definitions: Essays in Contemporary Criticism.* Second series. New York: Harcourt, Brace and Co., 1924.

Cannadine, David. "On Reviewing and Being Reviewed." *History Today,* March 1999, 30–33.

Charles, Ron. "Will Authors Get Honest Review for $350?" *Christian Science Monitor,* September 27, 2004, 12.

Ciabattari, Jane. "Editors on Reviews." *Poets and Writers,* July/August 2003, 48–55.

Clurman, Harold. "A Critic's Credo." *Nation,* September 14, 1964, 120–22.

Coleman, Wanda. "Hunt and Peck: Book Reviewing, African-American Style." *L. A. Weekly,* August 9–15, 2002, www.laweekly.com.

Complete Review Quarterly. "Withering Reviews: Where Have All the Book Reviews Gone?" *Complete Review,* vol. 2, issue 2, May 2001, www.complete-review.com.

Conason, Joe. "The Woman Who Couldn't Read." *Salon,* January 27, 2003, www.salon.com.

Connolly, Cyril. *The Selected Essays of Cyril Connolly.* Edited and with an introduction by Peter Quennell. New York: Persea Books, 1984.

Constantine, David. "Eager to Come at the Truth." Review of *Behind the Lines,* by Michael Hofmann, and *Signs and Wonders,* by D. J. Enright. *Times Literary Supplement,* November 16, 2001, 12.

Cook, Bruce. "The Select and Sought-After Newspaper Book Sections." *Washington Journalism Review,* May 1983, 24–29.

Cooper, Arthur. "Critic as Superstar." *Newsweek,* December 24, 1973, 96–98.

Cooper, Gloria. "Dart to Tulsa World." Darts and Laurels. *Columbia Journalism Review,* November/December 1991, 38.

———. "Book Reviewing Ain't Beanbag." Darts and Laurels. *Columbia Journalism Review,* July/August 2000, 14.

Coser, Lewis A., Charles Kadushin, and Walter W. Powell. *Books: The Culture and Commerce of Publishing.* New York: Basic Books, Inc., 1982.

Cotts, Cynthia. "Boy, Girl, Boy: Sexism at the *NYT Book Review*?" Press Clips. *Village Voice,* January 7–13, 2004, www.villagevoice.com.

Cox, Ana Marie. "The Soft Bigotry of Low Expectations." *the antic muse,* May 9, 2003, www.theanticmuse.com.

Davidson, Donald. "Criticism outside New York." In *The Spyglass, Views and Reviews, 1924–1930.* Selected and edited by John Tyree Fain. Nashville: Vanderbilt University Press, 1963. Originally published, in slightly different form, under the title, "Provincial Book Reviewing." *Bookman,* May 1931.

Davis, Elmer. *History of the* New York Times, *1851–1921.* New York: New York Times, 1921.

Diamond, Edwin. *Behind the Times: Inside the New* New York Times. New York: Villard Books, 1994.

———. "Can You *Prove* the Hollandaise Was Curdled?" *New York Magazine,* April 18, 1994, 32, 34.

Dobrzynski, Judith H. "Embarrassment of Critics: Raters Rated." *New York Times,* June 20, 1998, A15, A17.

Dorris, Michael. "Say, Who Was That Semi-Masked Book Reviewer?" *Boston Sunday Globe,* December 8, 1991, A14.

Dreher, Christopher. "Bribes, Threats and Naked Readings." *Salon,* September 16, 2002, www.salon.com.

Drewry, John E. *Writing Book Reviews.* Boston: The Writer, Inc., 1966.

Eisenberg, Howard. "So Many Books, So Little Space." *Publishers Weekly,* April 10, 1987, 25–30.

Epstein, Joseph. "Reviewing and Being Reviewed." In *Plausible Prejudices.* New York: W. W. Norton, 1985.

Fialkoff, Francine. "Tainted Reviews." *Library Journal,* June 15, 2001, 61.

———. "What's a Review, Anyway?" *Library Journal,* July 2001, 72.

Fields, Howard. "Libel Suit over *N. Y. Times* Book Review Is Reinstated." *Publishers Weekly,* March 7, 1994, 14.

Fleming, Thomas. "The War between Writers and Reviewers." *New York Times Book Review,* January 6, 1985, 3, 37.

Frizzelle, Christopher. "Rant! The Rise of the Critical Critic." *Seattle Weekly,* September 5–11, 2002, www.seattleweekly.com.

Funderburg, Lise. "Authors on Reviews." *Poets and Writers,* May/June 2003, 42–53.

Fusilli, Jim. "A Crime Columnist's Confession: Reviewing Is a Rough Trade." *Boston Sunday Globe,* July 18, 2004, E7.

Fussell, Paul. "Vanity in Review." *Harper's,* February 1982, 68–73.

Gannon, Mary. "Critics on Reviews." *Poets and Writers,* September/October 2003, 54–61.

Garbus, Martin. "My Mother, Book Reviews and the First Amendment." My Say. *Publishers Weekly,* April 25, 1994, 28.

Gard, Wayne. *Book Reviewing.* New York: F. S. Crofts, 1937.

Gardiner, Harold C. "Fainting with Damn Praise." In *In All Conscience: Reflections on Books and Culture.* Garden City, N. Y.: Hanover House, 1959.

Garner, Dwight. "Crisis in Critville: Why You Can't Trust Book Reviews." (Also titled: "Blurbmania: When Good Reviews Happen to Bad Books.") *Salon,* May 3, 1996, www.salon.com.

Gissen, Max. "Commercial Criticism and Punch-Drunk Reviewing." *Antioch Review,* Summer 1942, 252–63.

Glendinning, Victoria. "The Book Reviewer: The Last Amateur?" *Essays by Divers Hands: Transactions of the Royal Society of Literature,* New Series: volume 44, edited by A. N. Wilson, 1986, 182–94.

Goodrich, Chris. "Book Reviews as Book Promotion." *Publishers Weekly,* September 21, 1984, 30.

Gorman, Trisha. "Which Books Should Get a Review? How Ten Magazines Choose." *Publishers Weekly,* November 6, 1981, 23–27.

Gould, Edward S. "American Criticism on American Literature." Lectures delivered before the Mercantile Library Association, December 29, 1835. New York: Printed for the Mercantile Library Association, 1836.

Greeley, Andrew. "Who Reads Book Reviews Anyway?" My Say. *Publishers Weekly,* April 10, 1987, 78.

Green, Jack. *Fire the Bastards!* Normal, Ill.: Dalkey Archive Press, 1992.

Griffin, Bryan. "Panic among the Philistines." *Harper's,* August 1981, 37–52; September 1981, 41–56.

Gross, John. *The Rise and Fall of the Man of Letters: A Study of the Idiosyncratic and the Humane in Modern Literature.* New York: Macmillan, 1969.

———. "The 'Littery Supplement' Comes of Age: A History, of Sorts, of the Book Review." *New York Times Book Review.* 100th Anniversary Issue, October 6, 1996, 9–10, 116.

Gutin, JoAnn C. "Becoming a Book Reviewer." *Writer,* October 1996, 18–20.

Hackett, Francis, ed. *On American Books: A Symposium by Five American Critics as Printed in the London Nation.* 1920. Reprint. Folcroft, Penn.: Folcroft Press, 1969.

Haines, Helen E. "Book Reviewing in Review." *Library Journal,* October 1, 1934, 733–37.

Hamilton, John Maxwell. "Inglorious Employment." In *Casanova Was a Book Lover and Other Naked Truths and Provocative Curiosities about the Writing, Selling, and Reading of Books.* Baton Rouge: Louisiana State University Press, 2000.

Hardwick, Elizabeth. "The Decline of Book Reviewing." *Harper's,* October 1959, 139–43.

Henderson, Bill, ed. Introduction by Anthony Brandt. *Rotten Reviews: A Literary Companion.* Wainscott, N. Y.: Pushcart Press, 1986.

Hoge, James O., ed. *Literary Reviewing.* Charlottesville: University Press of Virginia, 1987.

Hoge, James O., and James L. W. West III. "Academic Book Reviewing: Some Problems and Suggestions." *Scholarly Publishing,* October 1979, 35–41.

Hoggart, Richard. "Reviewers and Reviewing." In *Between Two Worlds: Essays.* London: Aurum Press, 2001, 132–41.

Hollander, John. "Some Animadversions on Current Reviewing." In *The American Reading Public: What It Reads, Why It Reads. The Daedalus Symposium, with Rebuttals and Other New Material.* Edited by Roger H. Smith. New York: R. R. Bowker, 1963.

Holt, Pat. "About Those 'Paid Reviews' from *ForeWord Magazine.*" Holt Uncensored, #242, June 12, 2001, www.holtuncensored.com.

———. "Those Dying Book Reviews." Part 1: "A World-Class Disgrace." Holt Uncensored #245, June 22, 2001; Part 2: "Patty's Great Idea." Holt Uncensored #246, June 26, 2001, www.holtuncensored.com.

Hoover, Bob. "Critic Blasts 'Snarky' Reviewers." *Pittsburgh Post-Gazette,* April 6, 2003, www.post-gazette.com.

———. "The Hunting of the Snarky Book Critic." *Pittsburgh Post-Gazette,* September 28, 2003, www.post-gazette.com.

———. "Bad Reviews Equal Bad Reviewers Is a Double Negative." *Pittsburgh Post-Gazette,* October 12, 2003, www.post-gazette.com.

———. "Where Does Book Criticism Go from Here?" *Pittsburgh Post-Gazette,* August 15, 2004, www.post-gazette.com.

Howard, Gerald. "The Cultural Ecology of Book Reviewing." *Media Studies Journal,* Summer 1992, 90–109.

Hower, Edward. "Reviewing Books." *Writer,* December 1993, 24–27.

Huang, Jim. "Wrong Man for the Job: An Essay on Reviewing." *Drood Review,* May/June 1996, www.droodreview.com.

James, Clive. "The Good of a Bad Review." Op-Ed. *New York Times,* September 7, 2003, 13.

Johnson, Dennis Loy. "How to Make Literary Journalists Nervous." *MobyLives,* April 2, 2001, www.mobylives.com.

———. "Vanity, Thy Name is *ForeWord*." *MobyLives,* May 21, 2001, www.mobylives.com.

Johnson, Greg. "Let's Give Reviewers Some Credit." My Say. *Publishers Weekly,* September 21, 1992, 104.

Joseph, Michael. *The Adventure of Publishing.* London: Allan Wingate, 1948.

Julavits, Heidi. "Rejoice! Believe! Be Strong and Read Hard! The Snarky, Dumbed-Down World of Book Reviewing." *Believer,* March 2003, 3–15.

Kamerman, Sylvia E., ed. *Book Reviewing.* Boston: The Writer, Inc., 1978.

Kelleher, James B. "The *Other* Book Review: L. A.'s Challenge to the *New York Times*." *Columbia Journalism Review,* March/April 1999, 10–11.

Kinsella, W. P. "Where the Hell Is the VP of Review Copies?" My Say. *Publishers Weekly,* February 24, 1992, 64.

Kirn, Walter. "Remember When Books Mattered?" *New York Times Book Review,* February 4, 2001, 8–9.

Kirsner, Scott. "Everyone's Always Been a Critic—but the Net Makes Their Voices Count." *Boston Sunday Globe,* April 30, 2006, D1.

Klinghoffer, David. "Black Madonna: Toni Morrison's Popularity Is Less a Matter of Literary Taste than of Mass Psychology." *National Review,* February 9, 1998, 30–32.

Kramer, Mimi. "Finally Free of Frank." *New York,* March 14, 1994, 46–50.

Kroll, Jack. "Who Shall Criticize the Critics?" *Newsweek,* January 21, 1974, 89.

Krystal, Arthur, ed. *A Company of Readers: Uncollected Writings of W. H. Auden, Jacques Barzun, and Lionel Trilling from the Readers' Subscription and Mid-Century Book Clubs.* New York: Free Press, 2001.

Leonard, John. "How a Caged Bird Learns to Sing; or, My Life at the *New York Times,* CBS and Other Pillars of the Media Establishment." *Nation,* June 26, 2000, 11–19.

Leonhardt, David. "Everyone's a Critic: Rating the Zagat Survey's Newfound Appetite for Cultural Clout." Arts and Leisure. *New York Times,* November 23, 2003, 1, 10, 25.

Lewin, Tamar. "In Reversal, Appeals Court Dismisses Libel Suit against *Times.*" *New York Times,* May 4, 1994, A21.

Lingeman, Richard. "Reviewmanship." *Nation,* December 22, 1984, 683–84.

Lyall, Sarah. "Partners in Interpretation." Book Notes. *New York Times,* March 23, 1994, C19.

Lyke, M. L. "When It Comes to Books, Everyone's a Cybercritic." *Seattle Post-Intelligencer,* January 27, 2000, www.seattlepi.com

McCombie, Brian. "Breaking into Book Reviewing." *Writer,* June 1996, 17.

McDonald, Florin L. "Book Reviewing in the American Newspaper." Ph.D. diss. University of Missouri, 1936.

Mailer, Norman. "A Critic with Balance: A Letter from Norman Mailer." *New York Times Book Review,* November 17, 1991, 7, 38.

Marx, Bill. "The Decline of Book Reviewing." My Say. *Publishers Weekly,* October 25, 1993, 36.

———. "Critical Condition." *Boston Sunday Globe,* April 21, 1996, 79, 81.

Mayer, Martin. "The Disembodied Voice of the Times Lit. Supp." In *All You Know Is Facts.* New York: Harper and Row, 1969.

Mayfield, Kendra. "Harriet the Online Book Reviewer." *Wired,* July 1, 2002, www.wired.com.

Mencken, H. L. "Criticism of Criticism of Criticism." In *Criticism in America: Its Function and Status.* Essays by Irving Babbitt, Van Wyck Brooks, W. C. Brownell, Ernest Boyd, T. S. Eliot, H. L. Mencken, Stuart P. Sherman, J. E. Spingarn, and George E. Woodberry. New York: Haskell House Publishers Ltd., 1969.

Mendelsohn, Daniel. "Nailed!" Review of *Hatchet Jobs: Writings on Contemporary Fiction,* by Dale Peck. *New York Review of Books,* July 15, 2004, 43–46.

Miles, Jack. "On Reviewing Popular Books." My Say. *Publishers Weekly,* July 27, 1990, 209.

———. "Can a Review Be Libelous?" *National Book Critics Circle Journal*, August 1994, 1–4.

Miles, Jack, and Douglas McLennan. "Biting Back at Toothless Critics." *Arts Journal*, www.artsjournal.com.

Miller, Laura. "How to Get on the Cover of the *New York Times Book Review*." *Salon*, July 29, 1999, www.salon.com.

———. "Book Lovers' Quarrel." *Salon*, October 26, 2001, www.salon.com.

———. "After Oprah." *Salon*, April 18, 2002, www.salon.com.

———. "The Hunting of the Snark." The Last Word. *New York Times Book Review*, October 5, 2003, 31.

———. "How Many Books Are Too Many?" The Last Word. *New York Times Book Review*, July 18, 2004, 23.

Milliot, Jim. "Booksellers Say Publishers Support Selling Efforts, but Could Do Better." *Publishers Weekly*, September 27, 1999, 12.

Miner, Valerie. *Rumors from the Cauldron: Selected Essays, Reviews, and Reportage*. Ann Arbor: University of Michigan Press, 1992.

Mott, Frank Luther. *A History of American Magazines*. 5 vols. Cambridge, Massachusetts: Harvard University Press, 1938–1968.

Myers, B. R. "A Reader's Manifesto." *Atlantic Monthly*, July/August 2001, 104–22.

———. "A Reader's Revenge." E-mail interview with Sage Stossel. *Atlantic Unbound*. The *Atlantic* Online, October 2, 2002, www.theatlantic.com.

Myers, D. G. "Whatever Became of Poet-Critics?" *South Carolina Review* 27, Spring 1995, 354–61.

Nathan, Paul. "Reviewers' Clout." *Publishers Weekly*, December 19, 1994, 17.

National Arts Journalism Program. "Bottom-Line Pressures in Publishing: Is the Critic More Important than Ever?" Panel discussion (edited and abbreviated), April 17, 1998, http://www.najp.org/publications/bottomline.pdf.

———. "Reporting the Arts II: New Coverage of Arts and Culture in America," 2004, http://www.najp.org/publications/researchreports/rta2.html.

National Book Critics Circle Journal, 1988–2005.

Norman, Michael. "A Book in Search of a Buzz: The Marketing of a First Novel." *New York Times Book Review,* January 30, 1994, 3, 22–25.

———. "Reader by Reader and Town by Town, A New Novelist Builds a Following." *New York Times Book Review,* February 6, 1994, 3, 28–30.

Okrent, Daniel. "The Report, the Review and a Grandstand Play." *New York Times,* June 27, 2004, the Public Editor, Week in Review, 2.

O'Rourke, Meghan. "The Wonder Years: When People Loved the *New York Times Book Review.*" Culturebox. *Slate,* December 2, 2003, www.slate .com.

Orwell, George. *The Collected Essays, Journalism and Letters of George Orwell.* Edited by Sonia Orwell and Ian Angus. 4 vols. Vols. 1–3, New York: Harcourt Brace Jovanovich, 1968; vol. 4, Harcourt, Brace and World, Inc. 1968.

Outland, Ethel R. *The "Effingham" Libels on Cooper: A Documentary History of the Libel Suits of James Fenimore Cooper Centering around the Three Mile Point Controversy and the Novel* Home as Found *1837–1845.* Madison: University of Wisconsin, Studies in Language and Literature, no. 28, 1929.

Payne, Tom. "Circle of Clichés: Tom Payne's Guide to the Words That Reviewers and Publishers Love Too Much." *UK Telegraph,* August 8, 2004, www.telegraph.co.uk.

Peck, Dale. *Hatchet Jobs: Writings on Contemporary Fiction.* New York: New Press, 2004.

Perry, Bliss. "Literary Criticism in American Periodicals." *Yale Review,* July 1914, 635–55.

———. "The American Reviewer." *Yale Review,* October 1914, 3–24.

Peyre, Henri. "What Is Wrong with American Book-Reviewing?" In *The American Reading Public: What It Reads, Why It Reads. The Daedalus Symposium, with Rebuttals and Other New Material.* Edited by Roger H. Smith. New York: R. R. Bowker, 1963.

Podhoretz, Norman. "Book Reviewing and Everyone I Know." In *Doings and Undoings: The Fifties and After in American Writing.* New York: Farrar, Straus and Giroux, 1966.

Pollitt, Katha. "Thank You for Hating My Book." Op-Ed. *New York Times,* July 12, 2006, A23.

Pool, Gail. "Inside Book Reviewing." *Boston Review,* August 1987, 8–10.

————. "Critics Unmasked: The Confidential Side of Book Reviewing." *Boston Review,* April 1988, 20–21.

————. "Too Many Reviews of Scholarly Books Are Puffy, Nasty, or Poorly Written." Point of View. *Chronicle of Higher Education,* July 20, 1988, A36.

————. "Magazines in Review," *Wilson Library Bulletin,* October 1992, 90–92.

————. "Eliminate The Negative? Reviewing, Censorship and Self-Censorship." *Women's Review of Books,* September 1994, 15–16.

Potter, Clarkson N. *Who Does What and Why in Book Publishing.* Secaucus, N. J.: Carol Publishing Group, 1990.

Press, Joy. "A Short Oral History of the *VLS.*" *Village Voice Literary Supplement,* October 2001, www.villagevoice.com.

Pritchard, William H. "Nasty Reviews: Easy to Give, Hard to Take." *New York Times Book Review,* May 7, 1989, 1, 36–37.

Prose, Francine. "Giveaways." Bookend. *New York Times Book Review,* August 6, 2000, 27.

Rapping, Elayne. "Growing Pains." *Women's Review of Books,* November 1994, 25–26.

Rawlinson, Nora. "The *New York Times Book Review* Blames Publishers." Editorial. *Publishers Weekly,* February 14, 1994, 6.

————. "A Change in the 'Forecasts.'" Editorial. *Publishers Weekly,* September 25, 2000, 9.

"Reviewing, Reviewers, Authors, Publishers, and Censorship." *Review of Contemporary Fiction.* Summer 1997, 251–64.

Rivers, William L. *Writing Opinion: Reviews.* Ames: Iowa State University Press, 1988.

Romano, Carlin. "Extra! Extra! The Sad Story of Books as News." *Media Studies Journal,* Summer 1992, 123–31.

————. "The *TLS:* A 100-Year Love Affair." Chronicle Review. *Chronicle of Higher Education,* March 8, 2002, B11.

Ross, Alan. "Successful Failures." Review of *Clever Hearts: Desmond and Molly MacCarthy: A Biography,* by Hugh and Mirabel Cecil. *Times Literary Supplement,* July 20–26, 1990, 770.

Rubin, Joan Shelley. *The Making of Middlebrow Culture.* Chapel Hill: University of North Carolina Press, 1992.

Russo, Maria. "When Authors Attack." *Salon,* March 2, 2001, www.salon.com.

Safire, William. "Blurbosphere." On Language. *New York Times Magazine,*
    May 1, 2005, 26.

Schlachter, Gail. "Reviewing the Reviewers." *RQ,* Summer 1988, 468–70.

Searing, Susan. "What Librarians Read." *Women's Review of Books,* Febru-
    ary 1995, 11–12.

See, Lisa. "The Great L. A. Poetry Battle." *Publishers Weekly,* May 29, 1987,
    52.

Shafer, Jack. "Fair Is Square: The Case for Hiring Biased Book Reviewers."
    Press Box. *Slate,* August 12, 2005, www.slate.com.

Shaw, David. "Papers' Stepchild: Reviewing Books." *Los Angeles Times,* De-
    cember 11, 1985, www.latimes.com.

———. "Power, Fear of *New York Times Book Review.*" *Los Angeles Times,*
    December 12, 1985, www.latimes.com.

———. "Choosing the Best of the Book Reviews." *Los Angeles Times,* De-
    cember 13, 1985.

Sheed, Wilfrid. *The Good Word and Other Words.* New York: Dutton, 1978.

Sheehan, Donald. *This Was Publishing: A Chronicle of the Book Trade in the
    Gilded Age.* Bloomington: Indiana University Press, 1952.

Shepard, Richard F. *The Paper's Papers: A Reporter's Journey through the
    Archives of the* New York Times. New York: Times Books, Random
    House, 1996.

Shulevitz, Judith. "The Best Revenge." Close Reader. *New York Times Book
    Review,* June 17, 2001, 31.

Sinkler, Rebecca Pepper. "Picks, Pans and Fragile Egos." *Civilization,* July/
    August 1995, 48–53.

Stevens, George, and Stanley Unwin. *Best-Sellers: Are They Born or Made?*
    London: George Allen and Unwin Ltd., 1939.

Sutherland, John. "Mightier than the Sword." *Guardian Unlimited Books,*
    December 9, 2002, www.guardian.co.uk.

Swinnerton, Frank, with notes by Frederic Melcher. *Authors and the Book
    Trade.* New York: Alfred A. Knopf, 1932.

———. *The Reviewing and Criticism of Books.* The Ninth Dent Memori-
    al Lecture. London: J. M. Dent and Sons Ltd., 1939.

Taylor, Jonathan. "Reviewers Who Love Too Much: A Critic Calls It Quits."
    Stranger, March 18, 1999, www.thestranger.com.

Teachout, Terry. "The Contrite Critic." OpinionJournal. *Wall Street Jour-
    nal,* editorial page, August 14, 2002, www.opinionjournal.com.

Thatcher, Sanford G. "A Call for a UP Review Medium." My Say. *Publishers Weekly,* December 28, 1992, 80.

Thompson, Charles Miner. "Honest Literary Criticism." *Atlantic Monthly,* July 1908, 179–90.

Tickle, Phyllis. "Raising the Brown Curtain." My Say. *Publishers Weekly,* June 27, 1986, 100.

Treglown, Jeremy, and Bridget Bennett, eds. *Grub Street and the Ivory Tower: Literary Journalism and Literary Scholarship from Fielding to the Internet.* New York: Oxford University Press, 1999.

Updike, John. Foreword to *Picked-Up Pieces.* New York: Alfred A. Knopf, 1975.

Waldman, Adelle. "Book Report: How Four Magazines You've Probably Never Read Help Determine What Books You Buy." Culturebox. *Slate,* September 12, 2003, www.slate.com.

Walker, Scott. "A Review in the *Times*?! Oh, No!" My Say. *Publishers Weekly,* October 11, 1993, 45.

Weber, Katharine. "The Reviewer's Experience." My Say. *Publishers Weekly,* February 15, 1993, 248.

Weinberg, Steve. "The Unruly World of Book Reviews." *Columbia Journalism Review,* March/April 1990, 51–54.

———. "The Kitty Kelley Syndrome." *Columbia Journalism Review,* July/August 1991, 36–40.

———. "Assigning Book Reviews: A System in Need of Repair?" *National Book Critics Circle Journal,* August 1993, 1–2.

Weisbard, Phyllis Holman. "Reviews and Their Afterlife." *Women's Review of Books,* January 1995, 16–17.

Weisberg, Jacob. "A Hundred Years of Lassitude: Will the *New York Times Book Review* Bore Readers for Another Century?" The Browser. *Slate,* November 15, 1998, www.slate.com.

Weschler, Lawrence. "Raising the Noise Level of Nonfiction Collections." My Say. *Publishers Weekly,* March 23, 1990, 57.

West, Paul. "The Twilight Double-Header: Some Ambivalences of the Reviewer Reviewed." In *Directions in Literary Criticism: Contemporary Approaches to Literature.* Edited by Stanley Weintraub and Philip Young. University Park: Pennsylvania State University Press, 1973.

———. "Deep-Sixed into the Atlantic." *Review of Contemporary Fiction,* Fall 1991, 260–62.

West, Rebecca. "The Duty of Harsh Criticism." *New Republic,* November 7, 1914, 18–20.

Wilmers, Mary-Kay. "The Language of Novel Reviewing." In *The State of the Language.* Edited by Leonard Michaels and Christopher Ricks. Berkeley: University of California Press, 1980.

Wilson, Edmund. *The Shores of Light: A Literary Chronicle of the Twenties and Thirties.* New York: Farrar, Straus and Young, 1952.

Winters, Stanley B. My Say. *Publishers Weekly,* April 26, 1985, 92.

Wolfe, Tom. "My Three Stooges." In *Hooking Up.* New York: Farrar, Straus and Giroux, 2000.

Wolper, R. S. "'A Grass-blade': On Academic Reviewing." *Scholarly Publishing,* July 1979, 325–28.

Woodcock, George. "The Critic as Mediator." *Scholarly Publishing,* April 1973, 201–9.

Woodward, Richard B. "Reading in the Dark: Has American Lit Crit Burned Out?" *Village Voice Literary Supplement,* October 1999, www.villagevoice.com.

Woolf, Virginia. "Reviewing." London: Hogarth Press, 1939.

Wyatt, Edward. "An Honest Book Review from *Kirkus*? Only $350." *New York Times,* October 5, 2004, B1, B7.

Wyatt, Robert. "Book Page Editor Blues." *Publishers Weekly,* September 21, 1984, 28–30.

Yagoda, Ben. "Michiko Kakutani: A Critic with a Fixation." Culturebox. *Slate,* April 10, 2006, www.slate.com.

Index

About the Author

Gail Pool is a freelance journalist and reviewer based in Cambridge, Massachusetts. She is a former editor of the *Boston Review;* she has been a book columnist for the *Christian Science Monitor,* the *Cleveland Plain Dealer,* and the *San Diego Union-Tribune;* and she is a member of the National Book Critics Circle. She is the editor of *Other People's Mail: An Anthology of Letter Stories* (University of Missouri Press).